# Praise for *Dealing with the Elephant in the Room*

"What a fantastic book! Mike Bechtle is not only entertaining and compelling but his advice is rock-solid and practical. Anyone who is serious about having healthy relationships—at work or on the home front—will love this book."

**Drs. Les and Leslie Parrott**, authors of *Saving Your Marriage Before It Starts*

"Mike Bechtle skillfully guides us to good communication skills. He points out that when we're under stress without the proper tools we usually default to toxic patterns learned in childhood— yelling, whining, or clamming up! Our body language, as well as our spoken words, can effectively calm our tough conversations or ignite a raging war. Being an effective communicator can be learned by using his easily applicable counsel. His book is full of wisdom."

**Elizabeth B. Brown**, author of *Living Successfully with Screwed-Up People*

# Praise for *How to Communicate with Confidence*

"Mike is a student of the art of communication. He will make a good teacher for every reader."

**John Ortberg**, author and pastor, Menlo Park Presbyterian Church

"Does anyone really know how to communicate well? Mike does, and this is a great tool to develop more intimate relationships and deeper connections in any situation."

ˌ ˌe **Arterburn**, New Life Ministries

D1383229

# THE PEOPLE PLEASER'S GUIDE TO LOVING OTHERS WITHOUT LOSING YOURSELF

# Other Books by Mike Bechtle

*Dealing with the Elephant in the Room*

*What Was He Thinking?*

*People Can't Drive You Crazy If You Don't Give Them the Keys*

*How to Communicate with Confidence*

*Evangelism for the Rest of Us*

# THE
# PEOPLE
## PLEASER'S
# GUIDE
## TO LOVING
# OTHERS
## WITHOUT
# LOSING
## YOURSELF

## Dr. Mike Bechtle

### Revell
*a division of Baker Publishing Group*
Grand Rapids, Michigan

Published by Revell
a division of Baker Publishing Group
PO Box 6287, Grand Rapids, MI 49516-6287
www.revellbooks.com

Printed in the United States of America

Library of Congress Cataloging-in-Publication Data
Names: Bechtle, Mike, 1952– author.
Title: The people pleaser's guide to loving others without losing yourself / Dr. Mike Bechtle.
Description: Grand Rapids, Michigan : Revell, a division of Baker Publishing Group, 2021.
Identifiers: LCCN 2020018623 | ISBN 9780800737870 (paperback)
Subjects: LCSH: Self-esteem—Religious aspects—Christianity. | Identity (Psychology)—Religious aspects—Christianity. | Love—Religious aspects—Christianity.
Classification: LCC BV4598.24 .B43 2021 | DDC 248.4—dc23
LC record available at https://lccn.loc.gov/2020018623

ISBN 9780800740382 (casebound)

In keeping with biblical principles of creation stewardship, Baker Publishing Group advocates the responsible use of our natural resources. As a member of the Green Press Initiative, our company uses recycled paper when possible. The text paper of this book is composed in part of post-consumer waste.

21   22   23   24   25   26   27        7   6   5   4   3   2   1

## To Averie

You are a masterpiece
God's poem
I watch you with amazement and joy
*You are enough*
Just the way you are

# Contents

# Introduction

## The Quest for Freedom

I was always going to let someone down, so I decided it
wouldn't be me anymore.

Unknown

I wrote this book because I was tired.

I've spent my whole life being a people pleaser. I didn't realize
it was happening because it had become so much a part of my
life—much like water goes unnoticed by a fish. I wanted people to
like me, and almost all my decisions were based on how to make
that happen.

When I was in high school, I felt insecure about myself (doesn't
everyone?). So when I first started working, I picked jobs that were
different from what my friends were doing: working in a morgue,
selling sheet music, running a commercial printing press, presenting a drive-time radio show, doing wedding photography, and so
on. I figured that people would notice what I did and would be
impressed.

It worked; they were impressed. But it didn't help me. Deep inside I knew that they were only impressed with what I was doing, not with who I was on the inside (or so I thought). I never gave them a chance to see who I really was because it was too risky.

I also made it a point to be "nice." I was attracted to people, especially adults, who were kind and agreeable and never got upset. They were consistent, and everybody liked them. I wondered why they never got angry about anything, and I assumed they just weren't angry people. So when I got angry, I learned to stuff it inside so nobody would know. I might be irritated at someone on the inside, but I'd say, "Oh, that's OK."

I wasn't OK. I became a counterfeit—but I believed it was essential to survival.

In other words, I was never my true self; I was a distorted mirror image of myself that I had created for others to see. This took a lot of work, because I could never let my guard down. My façade required constant vigilance. It had become my identity, and I was focused on keeping up that image.

I was a serial people pleaser.

## Searching for a Solution

Eventually, I started running out of fuel. I realized I was living for others instead of myself, but I felt trapped and didn't see a way out. I had trouble sleeping at night because my mind was racing with anxiety. I knew this wasn't sustainable and that at some point I would crash and burn.

I went to a bookstore to see what was available that might help and found a number of books to choose from. I flipped through most of them and found three common messages:

1. People pleasing is bad.
2. You need to stop being a people pleaser.
3. The way to stop is to focus on pleasing yourself, not others.

It kind of made sense but somehow didn't ring true. I felt like these books were telling me to become irritating and obnoxious to others and just pay attention to me. This seemed foreign to the person I had been my whole life. I wasn't an irritating person; I was a *nice* person. Did I have to stop being nice?

I read those books, then checked out different articles and websites—and found much of the same advice: *I needed to change my focus from meeting the needs of others to taking care of #1—me.* The more I read, the more I saw the same perspective. If this was true, my lifelong focus on others had been robbing me of myself.

I apparently needed to become more selfish.

But deep inside, nagging thoughts kept rising.

*Could there be a good side to being a people pleaser?*

*Could there be another, better way to feel good about myself than depending on what others think?*

*Could I still be a people pleaser if I developed a healthy view of myself?*

*Could I still care about others but do it from a place of confidence and strength?*

That's where my journey began. To answer those questions, I began exploring how to build a view of myself that wasn't based on the opinions of others. If I could see myself accurately and learn to accept my uniqueness, I wouldn't have to try to impress others anymore. I could just care about them.

And so, this book goes one step further than most of the others I've seen out there. It recognizes the negative side of being a people pleaser, when it's just a vehicle to build our own self-esteem. But it also recognizes there's a positive side to pleasing that comes from learning to focus on ourselves to become healthy.

If we can get to that healthy place, it provides a perfect foundation for being a "power" people pleaser. We can reach out to serve others and meet their needs—for the right reasons. We can truly focus on others because we're OK with who we really are.

## The People Pleasing Payoff

I wish I could say I'm writing this book in the past tense and that I've been completely healed from my lifelong struggle with people pleasing. Well, the tendencies are still there, and I'm not finished yet. But I've found a whole new level of confidence from being myself and capitalizing on that uniqueness to reach out to others. I'm on a journey, and I want to invite you to come with me so you can find freedom as well. I don't pretend to have all the answers; I just want to be your guide as you begin your own journey.

Think of this as a conversation over coffee. In each chapter, we'll meet to talk through different aspects of the process. We'll discuss what works and what doesn't and share stories of others who have wrestled with the same struggles. We'll also get practical—I'll help you develop your own step-by-step map to make it through the wilderness.

I have "Dr." in front of my name, but I'm not a psychologist. I won't pretend to give the valuable insight a therapist can provide. (I've experienced that value firsthand, learning about my motives and drives from professionals who know what to look for.) My doctorate is in higher education and adult learning, and I've spent my career in the classroom, both university and corporate, discovering how to negotiate the challenges of communication. That's the perspective I'll bring to the table—a practical approach to relationships, which has been the focus of all my previous books.

Here's what you'll gain from joining me in this journey:

- You'll realize that it's possible to break free from lifelong patterns (and it's not as hard as you think).
- You'll learn how to say no instead of automatically saying yes (no matter who's asking).

- You'll relax in real relationships instead of feeling the need to manipulate others (even when they're being manipulative).
- You'll find it easier to get people to like you by being real (and realize you're "enough").
- You'll learn to find yourself so you can learn to like yourself (without having to become someone you're not).
- You'll be less overwhelmed, since you won't be spending so much time positioning yourself in relationships (taking your hands off the controls).
- You'll become who you really are—and you can still be "nice" (or even nicer).
- You'll learn to handle conflict without intimidation (and do it with confidence).
- You'll have less anxiety and finally get that good night's sleep.

Bottom line: *there's hope.* You don't have to continue to struggle in the quicksand of pleasing others to build your self-esteem. But as you build a healthy foundation for yourself, you'll become a *real* people pleaser—in the best way possible! The more you please yourself, the more pleasing you'll be to others.

It might seem like an insurmountable task, like climbing Mt. Everest, especially if pleasing has been a lifelong pattern. But no one can climb a mountain in a single step. The only thing we can do is take that first step, then the next, then the next. Individual steps are easy—they just need to be repeated.

No one climbs a mountain by accident. It's intentional—and possible.

Ready to take the first step? Turn the page and let's begin the journey together.

# PART 1

---

# BUILDING
# A VISION

---

Which would you rather do?

a) Run a marathon.
b) Eat bacon (or another favorite food).

If you've developed a fitness habit, you might choose the marathon. It's a huge challenge and takes months of preparation, but it energizes you. You choose to do the hard thing because you're motivated by the result at the end.

But you're probably in the minority. For most of us, it's tough to make the choice to start a long run when we can smell our favorite food cooking. If we want to achieve a major goal, we'll have to learn to make short-term choices that might be somewhat painful.

That's why we go to the gym or take an early-morning run. It's not easy, but it's the price we must pay to reach the finish line.

Exercise is hard. Eating is easy.

Personally, I'd rather skip the run and eat bacon because it's pleasurable in the moment. But if my goal is finishing a marathon, it's the wrong choice. In the moment, there's no obvious consequence for most of our choices. When the immediate pleasure is strong enough, it's hard to resist since its outcome seems so far in the future. As James Clear writes, "The costs of your good habits are in the present. The costs of your bad habits are in the future."[1]

What would happen if we immediately gained ten pounds every time we ate a strip of bacon? As much as we might enjoy the snack, that immediate consequence would help us avoid it. But since that impact is postponed, we often make the easy choices instead of the hard ones.

Everybody wants to be happy and comfortable. We're hard-wired for it. That's why we seek pleasure and avoid pain. In the quest for happiness, we're always balancing on the tightrope between "present pleasure" and "future pleasure." We want to feel good about ourselves, and we instinctively do whatever we can to make that happen in the moment.

For people pleasers, it's easy to focus on the needs of others, because their positive response in the moment makes us feel better. That's why it's uncomfortable to shift our focus to our own needs—but that's what leads us to a healthy place in the future.

---

Let's ask another question: What would freedom look like? So far, we've looked briefly at what people pleasing is and the process that got us there. For the bulk of this book, we'll look at the specifics of the "recovery" process for becoming healthy while capitalizing on our desire to please others. But there's one more step that's necessary before we begin that journey: getting a clear picture of our destination.

What would it feel like to be free from constant concern over our image? How would we feel if we were secure enough on the inside to be able to serve others freely—without needing their approval?

It's like going on a cross-country trip by car. The first step is to determine where we want to end up. Once we've done that, we put the destination into our GPS or online map, and we receive several different routes to get there. One might be the fastest route, while another might be the most scenic. But none of it works without a precise destination. With no destination, we'll simply drive in circles.

We people please because we want to feel value. Somehow, we start looking to others to meet that need. If people like us, we feel we have value. But we have to keep people pleasing to continue feeling that sense of value.

This is the typical pattern of an unhealthy people pleaser:

- Recognize our need to feel valuable.
- Get that value from the opinions of others.
- Become enslaved to their opinions.
- Serve others for our own benefit, not theirs.
- Feel trapped.

Here's the alternate pattern we'll be learning in this book:

- Recognize our need to feel valuable.
- Get that value from the inside, from a sense of our own uniqueness.
- Listen to the opinions of others without using those opinions to critique ourselves.
- Serve others for their benefit, not ours.
- Find freedom.

Let's jump into the journey to understand exactly what people pleasing looks like in our lives and the impact it has on us.

# 1

# How Did We Get This Way?

> When a people pleaser dies, they see the life of someone else
> flash before their eyes.
>
> Unknown

You're strolling through a department store, shopping and enjoying the day. As you turn down an aisle, you catch a glance at yourself in a mirror. It catches you off guard, and you are shocked. *What? I look like* that? It might be your weight, your clothing, your hair, or your expression. But it's not what you were expecting, and you start beating yourself up with a downward spiral of negative self-talk.

*That's disgusting—I'm disgusting.*
*Other people are seeing what I see, and they're disgusted too.*
*I can't believe I've let myself go like that.*
*I look horrible.*
*I've made horrible choices to allow myself to get to this place.*

21

*I'm going on a diet or getting a makeover or plastic surgery
so I can change this.*
*I'll only eat celery for the rest of the day.*

You didn't plan your reaction—it just happened in a matter
of seconds. One moment, you weren't even thinking about it and
were having a great day. A few seconds later, your perception of
yourself had completely changed . . . all because of a mirror. The
mirror became a trigger.

You feel terrible as you walk out into the mall. You pass the
food court where you smell the fresh, warm cinnamon rolls bak-
ing, and you sense that one would make you feel better, so you buy
one. There's a reason they call it *comfort* food. Your first bite is
immediately satisfying—but then you realize what you're doing.
You feel even worse because you broke your celery commitment
before it even started.

Throughout your life, you've learned that a mirror is a tool for
finding truth. You use it in the morning when you're getting ready for
the day, making sure the image you present to others is exactly what
you want it to be. You use it in a dressing room to see how a piece
of clothing looks on you. Public restrooms have mirrors over the
sink so you can make sure you're ready to step back into the world.

We never question mirrors. We believe them. We never say,
"Wow—I don't really look like that. There must be something
wrong with that mirror." We assume the reflection is accurate.

It starts early in life. Studies have shown that babies begin to
recognize themselves in a mirror at around eighteen months.[1] But
they're not critiquing themselves based on that reflection; they're
just thinking, *Hey—that's me!* When somebody says, "You're such
a good-looking little kid," a child instinctively looks in the mirror
to see what "good-looking" looks like.

Over time, the mirror becomes a tool to analyze what others
have told us. If somebody says, "You have a black smudge on your
forehead," you look in the mirror to see if it's true. If it is, you do

what you can to remove the mark so people will still think you're "good-looking."

As children, we assume that what we see in the mirror is an accurate reflection. The older we get, the more we compare what we see in that mirror with what we *want* to look like. If it matches, we're OK. If it doesn't, we get discouraged.

*But what if the mirror we're using is wrong?*

## Bullied by the Mirror

Most county fairs have a "fun house" with exhibits that capture our attention or entertain us. One common attraction features a room full of mirrors that are distorted. One mirror makes us look tall and thin, while another makes us look short and wide. Others make our bodies large and our heads the size of a ping-pong ball. The next one might make our feet the size of a Volkswagen while the rest of our body looks like a stick figure. We laugh, because it's obvious the mirror is distorted. It's not real, and it doesn't make us want to eat cinnamon rolls.

Here's the problem: as kids, we learn to use other people as mirrors too. We trust their reflection of how they see us. Someone says something about us, and we assume it's accurate. Whether it's someone who cares about us or someone who dislikes us, we take their perspective as truth. If we start believing the opinions of others are as accurate as a literal mirror, they start to replace that mirror. That sets up a paradigm we carry into adulthood if we don't recognize it.

In reality, those opinions might be as credible as a fun-house mirror. The distortion should be obvious, but we forget that. Our opinion of ourselves starts to reflect what others think—or *how we think* they think.

That's an even bigger problem: people might not even be saying or thinking anything about us, but we assume they are. We project our own self-image onto them, figuring that if they see the same things we do, they must be judging us in the same way we judge ourselves.

Let's say we're trying to learn a sport like softball. We haven't gotten very good at catching balls that are hit to us, and we think, *I'm really bad at catching—and I let the team down every time I miss.* It becomes our truth, and we believe it. Nobody else says anything—but we assume they're thinking the same thing. We assume others are saying, "You're really bad at catching. You're letting us down." We take it further, thinking they're also thinking we're a bad person, and they don't want us on the team.

Nobody said any of those things, but we've projected it onto them. Now we're using them as a mirror—yet we're the ones who created the mirror. We assume that when others look at us, they're seeing what we see and thinking what we think. If we're critical of what we see in the mirror, we believe everyone else is critical too.

My wife and I have a magnifying mirror in our bathroom. We call it the "scary mirror" because it shows us things we don't see in a regular mirror. It's great when we're trying to remove a tiny splinter, but it shows every facial flaw in great detail. But we'd get into trouble if we looked in the scary mirror and assumed everyone else was examining us with that level of detail.

When we focus on such tiny imperfections, we'll always see ourselves negatively.

## It Starts Early

Babies don't start life as competent in anything. They can't feed themselves, change themselves, or meet their own basic needs. Somebody else has to do these things for them, or they won't survive. We don't feel badly about meeting those needs because we understand how the process of growing up works. It's our job to get our children started.

We assume that, over time, they'll start learning to do things by themselves. We don't expect them to be experts, but it's natural that they try things out and build their own skills. We're still involved, but they gradually learn how to meet their own needs. If that doesn't happen, it's outside of the norm.

Over the next couple of decades, we provide for them while expecting they'll begin to gain more and more ability to take care of themselves. As they develop those skills, we provide for them less and less. We transfer the ownership and maintenance of their lives over to them. The goal is for them to move into society being able to make good choices to meet their own needs.

Sure, there are individuals who are born with physical, mental, or emotional challenges and need a different level of care. But for everyone else, the growth process in those areas is expected. Physically, they learn to provide for themselves. Intellectually, they learn how to develop their own thinking skills. Emotionally, they learn to find security internally rather than from the opinions of others. It's a natural part of the growth process, and healthy.

That gives people a solid foundation from which to reach out and invest in the lives of others in a natural, healthy way. They're not looking to those people to build their own sense of self; they're free to interact with them without expecting anything in return. They see themselves through an accurate mirror, which enables them to see others clearly as well.

Some people don't make those transitions well. Maybe they didn't learn the skills of providing for themselves, and this follows them into adulthood. Maybe they were in an environment where they were taught *what* to think but not *how* to think—so they lack the capacity to discern and make confident choices.

That emotional area of development can be the most challenging. Healthy people grow up learning to be content with themselves. They're valued for who they are, not just for what they can do. They were raised in an environment of acceptance rather than performance. Their mirror is focused inward on who they really are rather than outward on the opinions of others. They develop the internal security to be able to analyze others' opinions accurately, and this security is their yardstick of truth.

Most people struggle in this area. We all have experiences with others that make us feel inadequate as we're growing up. If we're secure enough on the inside, we can discern whether that input was accurate or not. But if we're struggling with basic insecurity, we're looking in the wrong mirror. If our own mirror isn't working, we look to the fun-house mirrors of others to decide what's real.

When people have recently asked me, "What are you writing about?" I'd say, "I'm writing a book about people pleasing," and nine out of ten of them gave me the same response: "Boy, I sure need that." When I asked for more detail, they'd say something like, "I'm such a people pleaser. I'm always worried about what people think, and I give up what I really want so they'll be happy." This becomes a pattern for most people, and they wish they could find freedom. It's so firmly ingrained they don't see any way out.

## The Way of Escape

As I mentioned briefly, most books and articles I've studied focus on how bad it is to be a people pleaser. They point out what we're doing to ourselves, decimating our own lives to impress others. Keeping up a charade takes constant vigilance and saps our emotional energy.

The common wisdom from those books is to stop trying to make others happy and put all of that energy into pleasing ourselves. It sounds good on the surface. But in practice, it can be just as frustrating. When we're focused on ourselves and ignore the interests of others, we're building a selfish approach to life and relationships. We want to be happy, but it's hard when we're lonely. That's where focusing on ourselves can lead.

Is it possible to find our security on the inside instead of the outside? What would happen if we could look in an accurate mirror, see who we are on the inside, and take ownership?

It's a two-part process:

1. Find our value in our own uniqueness, not in the opinion of others.
2. Use that uniqueness to serve others.

We won't be serving others so we'll feel good about ourselves; we'll be serving them *because* we feel good about ourselves.

If we can build that solid foundation for our personal worth and security, people pleasing is no longer something to be avoided. It becomes a powerful tool for impacting the lives of others.

How can we make those changes? First, we need to discover what kind of people pleaser we are so we can determine what steps to take. We can discover the truth about ourselves—and what it means for the future.

# 2

# What Kind of
# People Pleaser Am I?

You are not required to set yourself on fire to keep others
warm.

Unknown

The longer you've been a people pleaser, the less you might realize
it. You've been doing it for so long it feels normal. I could ask,
"Are you a people pleaser?" and you might instinctively say "No."

You probably responded that way for one of two reasons:

1. You know you're a people pleaser, but you don't want me
   to think negatively of you. So you won't admit it, even
   though you know it's true.
2. You don't know you're a people pleaser. It's such a part
   of you that you don't realize it's happening. It's just your
   identity, and you can't imagine being any other way.

It's like the foundation of a house: you know it's there, but it doesn't enter your mind unless something goes wrong.

Every time we've purchased a house over the years, we did a walk-through before signing the final paperwork. We would see a ton of things that were wrong we committed to changing.

"That baseboard is so dated; we'll need to replace that right away."

"Those hinges are rusty; they have to go."

"The garage door barely works. It could be dangerous, so we need to replace it."

We'd move in, and it always seemed to take longer than expected to get unpacked and settled. Then we'd have to go back to work, and life would take over. All those things we were so anxious to take care of never seemed quite as pressing anymore, and we'd soon forget about them.

They'd still be there, but we just got used to them. We didn't notice them anymore.

This is a familiar pattern for long-time people pleasers. As kids, we look for the affirmation and approval of others. If that approval doesn't come, we find ways to make it happen. Then we keep doing those things that work until they become a habit. Over time, those actions grow into a full-fledged addiction, and we need a regular "approval fix." It's our drug of choice, and we can convince ourselves we're not addicted.

This is a tough one, because the outcome of the addiction is a noble one: service to others. We can easily justify what we do because it leads to something positive. The more we do it, the better other people feel. The better they feel, the more they might like us. The more they like us, the more we like ourselves.

But it's not their job to like us. It's ours.

## An Honest Look in the Mirror

The first step in any recovery process is to admit there's a problem. For a people pleaser, it's especially challenging because we want to serve others. But there's a difference between "serving people" and "wanting to be *seen* as someone who serves people." The first is healthy because it comes from a place of genuine care for others. The second is selfish and uses others to get our own needs met.

Let's start with clarity. We need to pull out the "scary mirror" to see the truth about our motives. Once we can see ourselves clearly and accurately, we can take the first step toward healing.

The following quiz is designed to reveal the degree of people pleasing you currently practice. Read each question and answer with your immediate response. Don't think too long about your answer. That's especially important if you're a people pleaser, since you've built a pattern of crafting responses to fit what you "should" say. It's critical to be as honest as possible, knowing that the goal is clarity—not impressing others.

Don't just tally your scores mentally as you go; grab a sheet of paper, number it from 1–30, and write down your response for each question. That allows you to go back and see which specific questions are the most revealing and where you want to focus your efforts to grow. If you're a people pleaser, you might feel threatened that someone might see your answers and think less of you. That's why writing them down separately (rather than in this book) is good; you can always shred your results when you're done.

Circle the appropriate answer for each question.

1. Do you regularly have anxiety, depression, headaches, stomach issues, or back pain?

   Always    Often    Sometimes    Rarely    Never

2. Do you avoid conflict so no one will criticize you?

    *4*        *3*        *2*        *1*        *0*

Always    Often    Sometimes    Rarely    Never

3. Do people say you're one of the nicest people they know?

Always    Often    Sometimes    Rarely    Never

4. Do you keep your negative feelings inside?

Always    Often    Sometimes    Rarely    Never

5. Do you say yes when you really feel like saying no?

Always    Often    Sometimes    Rarely    Never

6. Is it hard to imagine standing up for yourself because people might not like you?

Always    Often    Sometimes    Rarely    Never

7. Do you usually wonder what people are thinking about you?

Always    Often    Sometimes    Rarely    Never

8. Were you punished for showing anger as a child?

Always    Often    Sometimes    Rarely    Never

9. Would you consider yourself a perfectionist?

Always    Often    Sometimes    Rarely    Never

10. Do you feel guilty saying no?

Always    Often    Sometimes    Rarely    Never

11. Do you avoid journaling for fear someone might read it?

_4_      _3_      _2_      _1_      _0_

Always    Often    Sometimes    Rarely    Never

12. Do you have a hard time asking others for help?

Always    Often    Sometimes    Rarely    Never

13. Do you allow visitors to stay longer than they should?

Always    Often    Sometimes    Rarely    Never

14. Do you feel hurt when others don't show their appreciation for what you've done?

Always    Often    Sometimes    Rarely    Never

15. Do you lie to keep from being rejected or misunderstood by others?

Always    Often    Sometimes    Rarely    Never

16. Are you critical of decisions you've made in the past—is it hard to let them go?

Always    Often    Sometimes    Rarely    Never

17. Do you bury your feelings?

Always    Often    Sometimes    Rarely    Never

18. Are you overwhelmed with a never-ending to-do list?

Always    Often    Sometimes    Rarely    Never

19. Do you have a tough time making decisions on your own?

    4        3        2        1        0

Always    Often    Sometimes    Rarely    Never

20. Do you apologize even if you weren't really at fault?

Always    Often    Sometimes    Rarely    Never

21. Do you feel like you're getting trapped into being a people pleaser, and it's getting worse?

Always    Often    Sometimes    Rarely    Never

22. When people disagree with you, do you tend to soften your position?

Always    Often    Sometimes    Rarely    Never

23. Do you compliment people so they'll like you?

Always    Often    Sometimes    Rarely    Never

24. Do you come to work early or stay late so people will be impressed with you?

Always    Often    Sometimes    Rarely    Never

25. Do you compare yourself with others?

Always    Often    Sometimes    Rarely    Never

26. When someone complains about something, do you keep quiet if you disagree?

Always    Often    Sometimes    Rarely    Never

27. Do you only try things when you know you'll succeed?

*4*      *3*      *2*      *1*      *0*

Always   Often   Sometimes   Rarely   Never

28. Is it easier for you to give than to take?

Always   Often   Sometimes   Rarely   Never

29. Do you avoid complaining about poor service or quality?

Always   Often   Sometimes   Rarely   Never

30. Are you an image-conscious person?

Always   Often   Sometimes   Rarely   Never

Score your results using this scale, then add them up:

- "Always" = 4 points
- "Often" = 3 points
- "Sometimes" = 2 points
- "Rarely" = 1 point
- "Never" = 0 points

Here's how to interpret your score:

*Total score 91–120.* If you're in this range, people pleasing has become your lifestyle and identity. You might not even be aware of it, but you know how you feel—the toll it's taking on your health, your sanity, your emotions, and your relationships. You're dependent on how others perceive you. If someone doesn't hold you in high regard, you think it's your fault. As a result, you're probably exhausted, anxious, and even depressed. People might like you, but you believe it's only because you've crafted the image they're appreciating. If they really knew the "real you," they'd probably feel differently.

This is the stage of *identity*, where the need to please is overwhelming and defines who you are. The thought of doing anything differently seems impossible. Fortunately, there are simple practices you can learn that can help you see results quickly. You'll learn in this book how to become a world-class people pleaser, which happens when you find a solid internal foundation for your identity. When you're healthy, you'll be free to please others.

*Total score 61–90.* In this range, people pleasing doesn't completely define you—but you may be well on your way. You've been practicing the behaviors of people pleasing for a long time, and they've become the lens through which you view others. You might have a few people in your life you can be real with, but they're the exceptions. You're usually at the mercy of people's opinions, real or perceived. It might be the people in your life you're closest to whom you struggle with most, and you might be feeling resentful they don't appreciate you as much as you need. You're still spending a ton of energy trying to please others for your own benefit, and it's making you really, really tired.

This is the stage of *habit*. At this stage, your choices will determine whether you move into the identity phase or into a healthy lifestyle. Fortunately, the choices to move in the right direction are simple ones. Later in this book, you'll learn simple, practical steps to begin changing your relationships immediately.

*Total score 31–60.* If you're in this category, you still have a fairly realistic perspective on yourself. You can identify your people pleasing tendencies, and you can probably recognize why you practice them. It's still dangerous, because you're seeing positive results from others when you shape your image for them instead of being real. The more positive results you get, the easier it is to repeat those choices and build negative patterns.

This is the stage of *routine*. Now is the time to see the truth and act accordingly. This is the easiest stage to find healing, because you're in the early stages of an unhealthy way of relating to others. You'll make the same choices to take control, but you have the advantage of catching the disease earlier rather than later. You're a warm, caring person and enjoy reaching out to others, but you need to learn to take an honest view of your motives.

*Total score 0–30.* You might have a few people pleasing tendencies on occasion, but you have a healthy view of yourself. Your value isn't dependent on what others think or do, and you have the ability to process criticism as constructive feedback or an opinion to simply dismiss. If someone thinks you're inconsiderate or insensitive, you don't base your personal sense of value on that.

This is the stage of *health.* Some people just know how to push your buttons, though. You're fine with everyone else, but you might find yourself a bit intimidated by certain people in certain situations. The value for you will be learning to recognize what's happening in those situations, and what steps to take to keep control of your own identity and emotions. The steps in this book will be tools you'll keep handy when needed rather than something you'll start using right away.

| Score | Stage |
|---|---|
| 91–120 | *The stage of Identity* |
| 61–90 | *The stage of Habit* |
| 31–60 | *The stage of Routine* |
| 0–30 | *The stage of Health* |

## From Diagnosis to Prescription

So, how do you feel after seeing your score?

It can be unnerving to see ourselves honestly, especially if we've been deceiving ourselves for a long time. After all, people pleasing has been a defense mechanism, and it has served us well. The longer we present ourselves to others in a carefully crafted way, the more we begin to believe it ourselves.

I discovered that reality early in my speaking career. I use a lot of stories to make points when I speak, and many of them come from my own life experiences. When I first started, I would tell a story and notice the reaction of the audience. If there was no reaction, I wouldn't use that story in the future. If the reaction was positive, I would tell it over and over.

I unconsciously began to fine-tune my delivery of those repeated stories to get more of an impact. The story was accurate, but I was gradually embellishing the details a tiny bit to get a better response. Over time, my stories would get better and better and would get a bigger reaction. Every time I would tell a story, I would picture it in my mind and simply describe the scene as I was seeing it.

One day, as I told a story I had told many times and saw it in my mind as I talked, it suddenly hit me: the story was so far from the original that it was no longer true. I had gotten so used to the "new" version over time that I believed it was accurate. I thought, *I'm seeing the picture of the situation as if it were a video recording—but that's not the way it happened.*

I was believing a contrived version of reality.

As I was returning home that night, I thought through other stories that had grown over time. In a sense, I had been deceived— and I was the one doing the deceiving. I made a commitment that, in the future, all my stories would stay true to the actual event. That didn't mean I couldn't craft my delivery; I just wanted to keep my integrity intact.

Taking this people pleaser quiz is a little like forcing yourself to stand naked in front of a mirror. You might not like what you see, but it's essential to know the truth before making changes, just as a doctor does a careful examination and diagnosis before writing a prescription.

Where do you go from here? I'd suggest two steps:

- Think carefully through the results of the quiz, focusing on the description of your results. Get a clear picture of who you are, present tense. Decide how accurate those descriptions are, and what you might change to fit the real you.

- Go back through your answers. Spend time with each question you answered "always" or "often," and think through how it plays out in your life. When is it most true? How does it make you feel when you're able to acknowledge it?

Don't rush through this; take the time you need to explore and revisit it for a while. Gradually, you'll find clarity in your present situation. You'll be looking in a real mirror for truth, not a funhouse mirror to impress.

Then work your way through the remaining chapters in this book. We'll develop a customized prescription you'll be able to follow back to a healthy perspective. The best part is that you'll find the steps are surprisingly simple—as long as you've started with truth.

What do we do next after we've discovered how we really relate to others? When the process feels overwhelming, and we've lived with this way of thinking for a lifetime, how can we find hope for the future? How can we escape and find wholeness?

It starts with a clear vision for the "future you." That provides a direction—and then we'll learn a practical process for getting there.

# 3

# How to Spot a Counterfeit

I gotta go. I have someone I have to be.

Unknown

Do any of these situations sound familiar?

- You're in the front of a crowded elevator, headed for the lobby. The door opens, and you step off—but you realize you're on the wrong floor. Everyone is watching. Do you get back on or let the doors close and wait for the next one?
- The office sets up an online crowdfunding page for a colleague with a new baby. You want the person receiving the gift to know you contributed, but the amount becomes visible to everyone when you do. You were planning to give ten dollars, but you notice everyone else is giving at least twenty-five. Do you change the amount you were

planning to give, stick with the smaller amount, or stay anonymous?

- You swipe your credit card for your coffee purchase, then the clerk spins the computer screen around so you can select the amount of your tip. The service wasn't great, so you'd prefer to give little or none. But they'll instantly see your selection. Would you give what you felt they deserved, knowing they'll see it? Or click on the larger amount?

- When you enter a single-person restroom in a restaurant and lock the door, you see there's a huge mess. Someone then jiggles the locked door handle, so you know they'll notice when you exit. You don't want them to think you made the mess, but it's not your job to clean it up. What would you do?

- Your friends chose a great restaurant that's known for their amazing desserts. You've been looking forward to trying one. But when the server asks if you'll be having dessert, everyone else at the table says, "No, thanks; we're fine." Would you order anyway?

There's a common theme between all these situations: fear of what people will think of us. We like to think we'd have the courage we need in these situations. But in the middle of them, it can be tough to make the decision we really want to make.

Why? Because we believe people will criticize us if we do, whether they say it out loud or not. For a people pleaser, that's unacceptable—and almost impossible to resist. So we avoid the uncomfortable, risky conversation now and agree to things we regret almost instantly.

As Robert Quillen said, "We buy things we don't need with money we don't have to impress people we don't like."[1] It's like putting our lives on credit—making painless choices now that we'll be paying for far into the future.

## We're Just Not Enough

We all want to feel good about ourselves. It's the foundation for everything we do. If we feel confident and secure, we're more likely to accomplish great things. If we feel inferior and insecure, we get stuck. Nothing else seems to work in life if we feel "broken" because our outer self conflicts with our inner self.

When we form our view of ourselves from the opinions of others, we believe what they say about us. Even if they don't say anything out loud, we assume we know what they're thinking—and it's almost always negative.

Sound familiar? We believe the negative much more quickly than the positive. When someone says something negative about us, we accept it as truth. But when someone says something positive, we assume they're just flattering us or don't really know us. We discount their affirmation but overemphasize their criticism.

## The Making of a Counterfeit

That's the problem with the slogan "Sticks and stones may break my bones, but words will never hurt me." We can recover from broken bones, but verbal wounds can impact us for a lifetime. They cut deep, and they form a foundation that shapes our mindset in every situation.

We decide that the best way to feel good about ourselves is to get others to like us. So we craft an image we think they'll appreciate. We ignore our uniqueness, thinking it's not enough. We give up what we want and give them what they want. We focus all our energy on being seen as helpful. And interested. And, well, *nice.*

That's a problem. We're not striving for our own happiness anymore—we're striving for their happiness instead of our own. One person has only enough energy to work on themselves. If we constantly try to make others happy as well, we'll run out of steam and be exhausted.

When we're growing up, we're not exactly sure how to make others happy. So we look for a role model, someone who's already doing it. We find someone who seems to be liked by everyone and gets positive reactions. We study their characteristics and try to emulate their attitudes, their actions, and their words. We think, *If I can just do what they do, everybody will like me too.* Gradually, we give up being ourselves and start becoming someone we're not.

That's where the downward spiral begins. Once we've convinced ourselves we need to be someone we're not, we begin crafting a fantasy. It's not real, but we try to convince everyone else it's true. We're copying someone else, and eventually we lose ourselves. We begin to believe the story we've created—the hollow image.

We've crafted a counterfeit.

It works for a while, because we get positive reactions from others. That feels good, but deep inside we know they're not reacting to the "real" person, so their accolades become meaningless. We sense that if they knew who we really were, they wouldn't like us or approve of us. We live our lives in a costume we never take off.

## The Value of a Counterfeit

Living a counterfeit life is a lot like owning counterfeit money. It's not real, but it sure looks like it. It could be in our wallet and we'd never realize it. But if we studied it closely, we would discover that it's worthless.

When we craft our image for others, we learn to hone our skills of counterfeiting. Our early attempts might look crude and obvious, like printing a dollar bill from a copy machine. It looks a little like currency, but we immediately know it's a fake.

Since our goal is to trick people into thinking that our image is real, we practice continually to perfect our craft. We learn what people respond well to, and then work hard to present that image. The more we do it, the better we get at positioning and posturing and fabricating the truth. We don't say, "What do you think of this fake image I'm projecting?" We just look for their reactions, using them as a mirror. We're basing our value on how people respond, passing out counterfeit bills and hoping nobody discovers they're not real. There's a lot we can learn from the characteristics of counterfeiting.

*Counterfeiters are precision engineers, not artists.* They're not trying to be creative or expressive, changing the colors or artwork on currency. They're trying to be as precise as possible to trick people into thinking it's the real thing.

*A counterfeit implies that there's something real.* By definition, a copy isn't original. It's a duplication of the real thing, which means the real thing exists. The counterfeit is fiction; the real thing is nonfiction. It's like people who avoid church by saying, "It's full of hypocrites." Their presence shows there's something real that people are being hypocritical about.

*The more valuable the original, the more time is spent on the copy.* Counterfeiters spend more time on making a fake $100 bill look real than a $1 bill. Because of the amount of time and precision it takes to make realistic counterfeit, they don't worry about low-denomination bills. That's why retail stores examine $100 bills to see if they're genuine but not $1 bills. The risk of loss is one hundred times greater. The more value the original has, the greater care is given in making the copy. That's why being a people pleaser can be exhausting; it takes a lot of work to perfect the image so people think it's real.

*To spot a counterfeit, study the real thing.* A bank executive I worked with told me that when they're training their tellers, they have them constantly handling real money. They become so familiar with the way it feels that they can usually spot a counterfeit simply by touch. They've studied the details so closely that it becomes obvious when they're holding a fake.

## People Pleasing—The High Payoff and the High Price

Maybe you're a people pleaser. If not, you probably know one. But you don't know their motives or how pleasing others might be draining their souls. You just know them by their positive characteristics.

- They're simply the nicest people you'll ever meet. Every time you encounter them, they're upbeat and encouraging.
- You don't ask them to do things for you very often, but from past experience you know they will always say yes. You can count on them to be there for you.
- They're always interested in what's happening with you and rarely focus on themselves. In fact, if you ask them personal questions, they'll answer quickly then turn the conversation back around to you.
- They're dependable. They always get their work done, and it's always on time.
- They're always available to help others and are usually the first to volunteer. They often sense a need you have even before you have said anything and volunteer to jump in.

Sounds great, doesn't it? They make a positive impact on everybody they meet, so it's easy to want to be like them. If we're struggling with our own security, they become our model of what we want to be like. That's OK, as long as that desire comes from a healthy place. It's "who we want to be when we grow up," and exemplifies what a life of effectively engaging with others looks like.

But if we're only looking on the surface, we don't really know what's happening on the inside. For an unhealthy people pleaser, their inner demons are probably hidden.

- They never miss a deadline but probably complete the project with great stress and procrastination.
- They make plans to take care of themselves but sacrifice self-care to the priorities of others.
- They believe they're not worthy of someone's love and acceptance.
- They might be loved by some people (or even most people), but it's not enough. If even one person doesn't affirm them, they'll do whatever they can to turn that person around.
- They'll go to great lengths to maintain relationships, giving up their own boundaries if they sense someone disapproves of them.
- They feel selfish doing anything for themselves.
- They don't like themselves for giving in so much and aren't attracted to people who are like them (they see those people as weak).
- They lose their sense of identity because they've hidden their true selves from others for so long.
- They become experts at dishonesty and deception since they need to hide the truth about themselves.
- They tend to be perfectionists who always follow the rules (at least outwardly).
- They feel like a failure if someone is unhappy with them.

*Urban Dictionary* defines a people pleaser as "a person who believes they are less than most others on the planet, and have the need to hide these beliefs from all whom they come in contact with."[2] So the image we present to others is like a Hollywood movie set where everything looks perfect, but it's only fake building fronts held up by scaffolding. We're so busy painting the façade that we don't have time to build the structure and furnish the interior. It looks great, and people are impressed. But it never gives us what we really need because we know people are responding to the image, not the reality.

We all want to be accepted by others, and we go to great lengths to make it happen. We can see that in the purchases we make, spending more money for cars, clothes, and clubs so others will be impressed.

But since they're doing the same thing, they're probably not noticing us anyway.

# PART 2

# FEAR FACTORS

In recent years, escape rooms have become a popular group activity. People go to a location where they're "locked" into a themed room (prison cell, cave, operating room, and so forth) and have to find their way out in a certain period of time. The solution is never obvious and can only be discovered as team members work together and strategize possibilities. They explore, find clues, and solve puzzles to find the "key" to escaping.

At first, the solution seems impossible. And usually it still feels that way even after thirty or forty minutes. Some team members are energized by the quest. Others decide it's hopeless and quit trying. They wait until the end of the game for someone to come get them, knowing they've lost.

There's always a way out; it's just not obvious and takes strategic thinking and cooperation with others.

This is not that different from being a people pleaser. Most people pleasers have been that way for their entire lives. They're in an escape room called "life." They've moved in, and the game never ends. They see others who find a solution, but they feel trapped and have given up hope of escape. They hate the game but keep playing. They want to get out but don't know how—and fear keeps them from trying.

What are they afraid of? It could be several things, but here are the five prominent fears of a people pleaser:

1. I need you to like me—*fear of rejection.*
2. I need you to not be angry with me—*fear of conflict.*
3. I need you to notice me—*fear of invisibility.*
4. I need you to affirm me—*fear of inadequacy.*
5. I need you to need me—*fear of irrelevance.*

Almost every book I've read on people pleasing says we should focus on our own needs instead of the needs of others. To some degree, that will work. But it's putting a bandage on the symptom and ignoring the real problem. We'll feel better at the expense of compassion while assuming our people pleasing tendencies are something to be eradicated.

Not dealing with those fears is like having a basement full of cockroaches. We can close the door and seal it so they don't come into the kitchen anymore. We'll clean and decorate the house and have dinner parties, but we know the roaches are thriving and multiplying in the dark. We're always worried they'll find another way into the rest of the house.

The only healthy approach is to treat the real issue first, which is understanding and dealing with the fears that keep us trapped. That's how we get out of the escape room. Once we've found freedom, we can begin the process of becoming world-class people pleasers. We'll be able to deeply impact the lives of others because we're no longer bound by our own fears.

Healthy people pleasers can change the world, and it starts by dealing with the cockroaches—the fears that keep us trapped. When we shine the light on them, they scatter. Some can be dealt with by understanding them and making different choices. Others might need a professional exterminator—a counselor or therapist who's an expert.

Let's open the door together and see what's in the basement. I'll bring the spray, you bring the flashlight.

It's time to deal with the bugs.

# 4

# I Need You to Like Me

## Fear of Rejection

Don't be afraid of your fears. They're not there to scare you.
They're there to let you know that something is worth it.

C. Joybell C.[1]

I asked a girl I didn't know very well out to homecoming in high
school. She said no.

It was out of character for me to ask, because I was allergic
to rejection (or at least it felt that way). I never took risks unless
I was sure someone would say yes. The few times I had been rejected growing up were painful, and I couldn't take a chance on
it happening again.

But my life was boring. I didn't have to suffer rejection, but I
never saw success either. There was no pain but also no gain. I
lived a beige life.

Maybe that's what caused me to take a risk this time. On the
one hand, I was terrified she would ridicule me for even asking.

But on the other hand, I had to try. I was sure she wouldn't go with me, but if I didn't ask, I was making that decision for her.

I didn't think she had a boyfriend, and it never occurred to me that she might already have a date (though homecoming was the next day). I knew she was one of the school cheerleaders, but I didn't realize she was in the homecoming court. There was a chance she could have been chosen as homecoming queen. If I had known that, I would have talked myself out of asking.

I built up my courage and made the call. I have no memory of what I said when she answered, but it was probably an awkward invitation. I do remember waiting for her response, bracing myself for the inevitable rejection.

She said no. But she did it so graciously it didn't hurt. She talked about already having plans with her family to go out after the football game and thanked me profusely for asking her. It might have just been an excuse, but she was known for her integrity, so I assumed she was telling the truth.

Rejection doesn't usually happen that way, though. It's often traumatic, and the pain lasts for a long time—possibly for a lifetime. We are kept from going after our dreams because we fear someone might reject us. We become paralyzed about moving forward because we don't want to feel that pain again.

It's one of the reasons we become people pleasers. We can't bear the thought of rejection, so we make sure there's nothing people can reject. We do that in two ways.

- We never ask for anything (so they can't say no).
- When we are asked for anything, we always say yes (so they won't be disappointed).

## Normalizing Rejection

Rejection doesn't usually stop us from taking risks; *fear of rejection* does. It's not the reality but the possibility that blocks us. It happens in our minds. We see ourselves in a certain way, so we assume others feel the same. We become amateur mind readers with no basis in fact.

Rejection is a normal part of life. Not everyone will say yes to us, and it's natural to be nervous when taking a risk. We may be turned down for several jobs before someone hires us. We make sales calls to many people before someone makes a purchase. We express opinions that others might not agree with.

For healthy people, rejection is a disappointment they learn to handle. For a people pleaser, it can become a crippling commentary on their personal value. When other people become our mirror of truth, we're at the mercy of their opinion. When they reject our contribution or request, they're not just telling us no; we hear it as a critique of our personhood.

If we can learn to reframe rejection, we can learn to accept the disappointment we feel and move forward. It no longer paralyzes us; it's simply another step in the process of growth and maturity.

Years ago, I read an article about a man who considered becoming a published author, writing articles for popular magazines. This was before the internet and email, so you would submit an article idea through the regular mail. You would send it off and include a self-addressed stamped envelope so an editor could use it to send you one of two things: an "acceptance letter" saying they wanted your article, or a "rejection slip," which was often a preprinted piece of paper saying they didn't want it.

This man was convinced he wasn't a good enough writer and would never get published. But he decided to make a game out of it, to see how many rejection slips he could collect by sending his ideas to editors. Each time he received a rejection slip, he would glue it to the wall of his tiny writing office. His goal was to wallpaper his entire office with rejection slips.

He sent off his first idea to an editor. About two weeks later, he received a polite rejection, which he immediately glued to his wall. He kept submitting to different magazines, and they kept rejecting him. He was pleased that in the first couple of months he already had seven rejection slips on his wall. He was making progress faster than he expected and was motivated to keep going.

But then the unthinkable happened: an editor bought one of his ideas. It was a blow to his plan, but he tried to see it as just a temporary setback. The fact they sent him a check for the article made it a little easier to handle his disappointment, though.

He kept submitting and getting rejected. But then he received another acceptance after only six more attempts.

You can guess how this turns out, right? He kept submitting and kept getting rejected. But in the meantime, his writing improved because of all the practice he was getting by writing and submitting. He got more and more acceptance letters and fewer and fewer rejections. He never finished his wallpaper job and spent the rest of his career as a full-time freelance writer. But even then, he continued to get rejection letters. They didn't mean he was a failure; those letters meant he kept trying, and they were a natural part of success.

I've gotten a ton of rejection slips in my career, and I still do. I found them tough in the beginning, because they would say something like, "Thank you for your submission. Unfortunately, this does not fit our editorial needs at this time." Most writers, including myself, read this as, "You're a horrible writer and should never submit anything ever again." The letter was rejecting my work, but I took it as rejecting *me*.

What if we could learn to take rejection as an expression of someone's opinion, without making it a judgment of our character? Rejection would no longer be something to fear, because it's simply another person's perspective. As long as we recognize that it says something about them and their view rather than about us, we'll be free to be ourselves even when people critique what we've done. We tend to link our actions with our character (if someone rejects one, they reject the other). The other person usually sees them as separate.

Does that mean it doesn't hurt when someone rejects us? Not at all. Pain is part of the human experience, and it's normal. It's healthy to experience the pain, but it's unhealthy to avoid the inevitable rejection that will come to all of us throughout our lives.

## Manipulation and the Fear of Saying No

Here's where it gets tricky. If we people please in order to avoid rejection, we think we're protecting ourselves. In reality, we're making it easy for others to manipulate us. They sense we'll always say yes, so they phrase requests in a way that makes us feel guilty if we don't agree.

> "I want to find out who my real friends are on Facebook. If you want to stay connected, just respond with yes to this post."
>
> "During this reception, we want to make a video of your best marriage advice for the bride and groom. We'll come by each of your tables to film you in a bit, so be thinking of what you'd like to say."
>
> "Can you help me move into my new place on Saturday? My own family won't help because they're so selfish. But I know I can always count on you. OK?"

When we agree, we usually feel resentful because we really don't want to do it. But we are also angry because we didn't have the backbone to stand up for ourselves. It's a repeating downward spiral that leads to feeling trapped in our weakness.

Here's a good question to ask ourselves as a check on our motives before we respond: *Do I really want to do this, or do I want people to see me doing it?*

When we never risk rejection, we think we're protecting ourselves from pain. But there's a much higher cost.

- We miss new opportunities that could take us to some amazing places in life. Without some degree of risk, we end up stuck in our current situation. As the old adage says, "Nothing ventured, nothing gained."
- We keep our perspectives to ourselves, so we lose the chance to impact others and help them shape their thinking.
- We don't share our real feelings with family or friends, so our closest relationships become shallow.
- We can become the "fix-it" person for everyone. They come to us for everything, and we build a low-grade resentment that becomes a barrier to relational intimacy.
- We withdraw from others so we don't get hurt. But over time we end up alone because we've built walls to prevent connections.
- We miss living in the moment. It's like going on a blind date but only thinking about how we look and whether they like us instead of enjoying the encounter.

One of the keys to healing is to intentionally focus on what freedom could look like. That's where the magic happens, somewhere between focusing on the potential pain and the courage to make that pain worth the risk. If we can reframe rejection as a tool for growth, we can gradually learn to tolerate that pain. The more we do this, the more our confidence builds. When our confidence is strong, it helps us build genuine, honest relationships.

## Climbing Out

If you've felt the sting of rejection, it might seem impossible to ever embrace it in the future. If someone broke your trust, it's easy to simply mistrust everyone to protect yourself. Learning to normalize rejection as part of the human experience doesn't minimize the reality of that earlier pain. But that pain doesn't have to dictate your choices in the future. It's possible to chart a new course.

How can that happen? Here are some simple perspectives to start moving forward.

1. The human mind knows how to heal. When you're hurt, take the time needed to grieve. But always look ahead toward healing. Lean into the pain and do the work needed to fully experience it, and then lean fully into the healing process when it's time.

2. Rejection won't break you, but regret will. Rejection is an event that happens, while regret is a mindset that builds over a lifetime. We usually don't recognize regret until it's too late, and it is only avoided by having a proper view of rejection when it happens. As President Theodore Roosevelt said, "It is hard to fail, but it is worse never to have tried to succeed."[2]

3. Our lives are built around our thoughts, our feelings, and our actions. Don't let your thoughts and feelings run your life. You can think afraid and feel afraid, but you can still act with courage.

4. Trust your ability to take important risks. You're stronger than you think.

5. Rejection moves you closer to what you want as long as you "get back on the horse." Always have a mindset of getting up. As Frank Sinatra sang, "Take a deep breath, pick yourself up, dust yourself off, and start all over again."[3]

6. If you need others to like you to feel valuable, you're positioning them above you. If you learn to find internal validation, it puts you on the same level as them—not above or below. That's how real relationships work.

You might have avoided rejection your entire life, and it feels like there's no hope of change. The good news is that change is possible, and it's not by becoming a doormat. It's by reframing rejection through seeing the truth of what it really is. Sure, it hurts when it happens, but so does exercise. If seen accurately, pain becomes a critical tool for helping us shape our people pleasing skills.

Avoiding rejection insulates us from pain but also from an abundant life. We can make a mental shift—a choice to focus on the potential that's on the other side of risk. Former Senator Robert Foster Bennett said it well:

> It is not rejection itself that people fear; it is the possible consequences of rejection. Preparing to accept those consequences and viewing rejection as a learning experience that will bring you closer to success will not only help you to conquer the fear of rejection, but help you appreciate rejection itself.[4]

It's a fear that can be overcome with truth.

# 5

# I Need You to Not Be Angry with Me

## *Fear of Conflict*

Conflict is always the right thing to do when it matters.

Patrick Lencioni[1]

I've always been enamored with magic shows. From the time I was a kid, I'd watch magicians perform and think, *How did they do that?* I was always baffled, seeing something happen I knew was impossible. My rational mind told me it couldn't happen, but I couldn't explain what I saw. Though I knew it was a trick, I always had a sense of wonder.

A friend of mine spent several years as a professional magician. He did some pretty amazing tricks and would never give away his secrets. I asked him, "How can you make me believe something that's isn't true?"

He replied, "I can't. You do it in your mind. I've studied how your mind works, and I capitalize on that." He continued, "The magic isn't in the trick itself; it's in knowing how you'll perceive what's happening."

He described how vision plays a part. We assume we're seeing things accurately. But it's easy to distort someone's perception while making something appear real, as seen by the familiar Müller-Lyer illusion.[2]

At first glance, we assume the lines are different lengths, while in reality they're identical.

My friend told me that most of his tricks were based on the brain's inability to focus on everything that's happening. It prioritizes the data, deciding what's most important to focus on. While we're looking carefully for certain things, we'll miss other obvious things we're not focusing on.

A magician is a master of deception and distraction. So is a people pleaser—especially in situations of conflict.

People disagree and emotions run high. Put a people pleaser into the mix and things settle down. The issue wasn't resolved, but the pleaser managed to distract people so they focused on something different. There's no solution, but there's also no conflict (for the moment).

It disappears like *magic*.

## Avoiding Conflict at All Cost

Conflict is often the worst thing a people pleaser might encounter. It's risky; it threatens their personal value and worth, so it needs to be avoided. Here's the thinking behind that paradigm.

*My value comes from the opinion of others.*
*I need people to like me, so I need them to be happy with me all the time.*
*Conflict is the opposite of happiness.*
*If there's conflict, they might not like me.*
*If they don't like me, my value is threatened.*
*I have to become an expert at avoiding conflict to keep my value intact.*

People pleasers want close, intimate relationships. But they often define *intimate* as "conflict-free." Their game plan for developing that type of intimacy is to make sure nobody's upset with them—ever. They see conflict as the fastest way to destroy relationships, so conflict becomes unacceptable.

In reality, the opposite is true. The fast-track to intimacy is to lean into conflict, embrace it, and use it as a tool for relationship depth. Avoiding it is faster and more comfortable in the short term, but it's like eating candy all day. It tastes good, but over time your health will be compromised.

One researcher discovered that "increases in positive feelings in close relationships depends on enhancing intimacy rather than on decreasing conflict."[3] The very thing we look to for strengthening our relationships (avoiding conflict) does the exact opposite. One of the best ways to increase intimacy is simply to be honest about how we feel.

"But I'm just not comfortable with conflict," you say. "It's painful, and I would never be able to go there." Fortunately, that's only a mindset. It's trapping you, and it's not accurate. Leaning into conflict is a skill that can be learned. You can practice it in small bites and build your skills over time. As you do, you'll build your confidence while you grow closer to others in a genuine way.

If you've been avoiding conflict, the idea of suddenly jumping into it feels like diving into an almost-frozen pond in January.

We're not talking about suddenly becoming argumentative and obnoxious. We're talking about starting with taking tiny risks to be honest and building from there.

I had a friend who decided he was tired of being out of shape, so he went to the gym. That very first day, he lifted the heaviest weights he could possibly lift, ran on a treadmill as fast as he could for several miles, and tried out every machine he could find.

He couldn't move for days afterward because of the pain. His first day was also the last day he went to the gym. Every time he considered it in the future, he remembered what that experience felt like and didn't want it to happen again.

We think, *He should have started small and worked his way up.* It seems obvious, but what about when applied to conflict? Isn't that sort of pain the reason we avoid conflict? We've had enough negative results in the past to inoculate us against trying in the future. But just as the gym wasn't the problem, conflict isn't the problem either. It's our perception. We remember the pain and don't want to experience it again. Yet we need to start small.

There are no conflict-free healthy relationships. The only relationships that are conflict-free are those where genuine thoughts and opinions are being hidden (or we just don't care). Healthy conflict strengthens relationships because we're connecting at a deeper level, not just on the surface. It feels risky because our whole identity seems like it's hanging in the balance.

If we can get good at conflict, it can become our greatest strength. As people pleasers, we're held back by our inability to express our honest feelings. We position ourselves so others will have a positive impression of us. If we develop the skills of dealing with conflict effectively, we have the potential to have the healthiest relationships of anyone we know. People pleasing becomes our "superpower" because we're intentionally impacting the lives of everyone we meet, and it's coming from a place of honesty, vulnerability, and strength.

It's your chance to help others become vulnerable as well, because they'll see the value you've brought to your relationship with them. Your conflict management skills become contagious, which teaches others how to deal with conflict in a meaningful way. As a result, all of your relationships become more real and satisfying. You'll find the intimacy you were trying to get by avoiding conflict.

## The Source of the Struggle

People pleasing isn't genetic. Anyone who's had a baby knows they don't come out of the womb compliant, wanting to please everyone around them. They're selfish, and all they care about is getting their own needs met. As we all know, that's perfectly normal. No new parent ever thinks, *When are you going to feed me? How come I always have to feed you?*

As those babies become toddlers, their selfishness continues. At the same time, they're starting to discover that other people respond to the things they do. In a healthy situation, they learn that they're loved and valued just for who they are, not for what they do. Their parents might become angry or frustrated with their behavior, but that conflict doesn't destroy their self-worth.

In an unhealthy situation, parents might have uncommonly high expectations of them and be overly critical, impose tough rules, withhold love and approval, or punish the child for making a mistake or showing anger. In that situation a child feels a sense of anxiety; it's not safe to be themselves. That begins a pattern that impacts all future relationships.

That pattern of avoiding conflict could also come from having aggressive siblings. If parents don't intervene and set boundaries, the kids don't learn skills of handling conflict and their sense of value is impacted.

Also, when parents' discipline and behavior are unpredictable, kids learn to be "good" to stay out of trouble. Over time, they experience conditional acceptance. The way to survive is to make sure nobody gets upset with them.

What does that look like as they move through life? Avoiding conflict becomes the filter through which they handle every life situation. As adults, they display these people pleasing behaviors:

- They're characterized by never-ending niceness.
- They're experts at changing the subject when things get tense.
- They want people to see them as even-tempered and kind.
- When others are in conflict, they engage in "fight or flight" and try to diffuse the tension or leave the situation.
- They pretend to care about people they really don't care about.
- They repress their honest feelings and keep smiling, even when they're in agony on the inside.
- They want to help people because they care, but it's more important that those people will think well of them.
- If a conflict starts that involves them, they'll find a way to postpone the discussion indefinitely.
- When tempers flare, they try to get everyone to calm down and talk rationally.
- They focus on the details instead of the real issue.
- They use humor to diffuse tension.
- They might be experiencing strong emotion, but they hide it so people won't see them as emotional or out of control. The result is that others think they agree since they're not sharing their opinions.
- They give in and let others have their way, even though they feel the opposite.
- They lie to protect their image.

Think about how this impacts everyday relationships, such as a marriage. Two people fall in love and get married. Before the wedding, they both had their own tastes, patterns, beliefs, and ways of looking at life. They made all their own choices. Up until now they've focused on the things they have in common.

Six months after the wedding they're each thinking, *Who are you, and what did you do with my spouse?* Not a lot has really changed, but they begin focusing on their differences. Those differences are normal and can lead to conflict.

Conflict is simply when two people think differently and have to figure out what to do with it. By that definition, it's a perfect opportunity for both people to grow as they talk through the issues. But if one person is a people pleaser, they see conflict as a threat to the relationship. They refuse to utilize conflict as the best available tool to strengthen their relationship. They think that if they're just "nice," it will diffuse the conflict and they'll become closer to the other person. In reality, such behavior only makes it worse.

## Battle Strategies

The more you get to genuinely know someone through times of conflict, the deeper you can go in understanding and empathy. Conflict is a road to connection, so it's worth learning to handle it well.

Entire books have been written about how to lean into conflict instead of leaning away from it. The purpose of this chapter isn't to provide a comprehensive course in making that transition; there just isn't space. Depending on how deep-seated our fear of conflict is, we might need the help of books, seminars, or even therapy to work through the issues.

Success is a matter of changing the way we think. Our goal is to see conflict through a new lens, recognizing how powerful it can be in developing intimacy in relationships. If we avoid it, we sabotage that intimacy.

What are some simple steps we can take to begin changing our mindset?

*Separate conflict from how people respond to it.*

When you bring up an issue and someone responds with anger or rage, that doesn't mean the conflict is bad; it's simply their response to the issue. Observe their reaction, then use their emotional response as a trigger to identify what the real issue is. That allows you to stay focused on the conflict without being shut down or intimidated by their emotions.

*Commit to speaking up when there's a conflict.*

You don't have to be an expert in debate or logic. Just find a way to simply state your opinion. The other person might react or attack your position ("How could you feel that way?"), but that doesn't negate your perspective. You're just trying to put your position out on the table instead of burying it because of fear of conflict. Without your opinion, there's no chance for a healthy, meaningful outcome.

*Realize conflict is normal.*

Practice moving into conflict instead of avoiding it. It's natural to want to wait until you've had time to ponder your perspective so you can present it with clarity, but it's best to bring it up quickly. Don't think about it too long—just tell the truth. Keep it brief, repeat it simply, and don't defend it. You're entitled to your opinion. If someone doesn't agree and tries to attack it, don't take the bait. Remember, you don't have to "win" the discussion; you're just sticking your toes in the water to experiment with engaging in conflict.

*Practice this in person.*

It might seem easier to share your opinions in writing or on the phone than in person. That's not necessarily a bad thing, but you want to build your skill to do this face-to-face. It's easier to say things in writing because we don't have to experience their reaction in the moment. But we're not trying to become better writers; we're trying to overcome our fear of conflict, which will only happen by being in the conversation where it's taking place.

### Slow down.

When emotions are high, logic disappears. Words can escalate, and we don't know how to respond. Instead of responding to comments when they happen, take a moment to carefully select your words. Not only will it allow you to select the most appropriate way to respond, but it changes the pace of the conversation to diffuse the energy that's driving it.

### Apologize simply when appropriate.

People pleasers tend to overapologize, taking everything as being their own fault. When appropriate, learn to apologize with one or more of these four phrases (possibly all four, in order):

- I'm sorry.
- I was wrong.
- I apologize.
- Please forgive me.

That's it. Adding a lot of detail weakens your apology.

### Pick your battles.

Ask yourself, *Is this really worth pursuing, or is it really not that important? Is this the best time and place to talk about this?*

### Communicate with precision.

- Explain your position clearly, and don't bring up anything from the past.
- Use "I" messages that don't put the other person on the defensive. Instead of "I hate that you never make the bed,"

you could say, "I feel overwhelmed when I have to make the bed every day."

- Check for understanding. "So, are you saying that when I (action), you feel (emotion)?" That gives them a chance to clarify if needed.

### Brainstorm for solutions.

Don't spend a lot of time going over the issue repeatedly. Move on as soon as it's appropriate to find solutions with the other person. Otherwise you'll both get stuck in the negative instead of moving forward.

## Digging for Diamonds

I was at a self-service car wash recently and pulled into the vacuum area. Right outside my door, someone had dumped their ashtray on the ground. I'm not sure what all was in there, but I don't think I want to know. There were cigarette butts and a few scraps of paper, but also a few coins and paper currency. They were all stuck together by a slimy, black, unidentifiable substance.

I'm guessing there was about five dollars in that pile. If I saw a five-dollar bill on the ground, I would pick it up. But in that disgusting mess, I wasn't about to touch it.

As I was vacuuming, I thought more about that pile. What if it were a $10 bill? Would I pick it up and clean it off? What if it were a $100 bill? When would it be worth it to dig out the cash?

The more valuable the cash, the more of a chance I'd go for it.

Conflict is like a diamond in a stinking pile of crud. For a people pleaser, everything inside them says to avoid it. But learning to lean into conflict is a diamond of great value for building world-class relationships. Sure, the situation might stink, and we don't want to go there. But the payoff is worth it.

Maybe it's time to start digging.

# 6

# I Need You to Notice Me

## Fear of Invisibility

Most days, I wander around feeling invisible. Like I'm a speck of dust floating in the air that can only be seen when a shaft of light hits it.

Sonya Sones[1]

My oldest granddaughter, Averie, is a huge fan of the Harry Potter book series. Young Harry and his friends attend Hogwarts, a school where they learn the skills of magic. As they acquire these new skills, they also pick up tools and resources along the way to help them handle a variety of challenges they face.

I began reading the books a couple of years ago. They're interesting, though I'm not quite as big a fan as Averie is. But I'm a huge fan of my granddaughter, so we've been able to read them together. (She's read the series seven times so far; I'm still working my way through the first time.)

We were having breakfast together one day, and Averie asked me, "Papa, if you could have any one tool that Harry and his friends use, which one would it be?" That was an easy one. "The invisibility cloak," I said. This was like a long, hooded gown a person could put on to become invisible.

"Why?" she asked.

I remember my reply. "So I could listen to what people were saying about me when they didn't think I was there."

We had quite a discussion after that.

Over the next few days, I thought about my answer. I realized that even as a child I dreamed of being able to become invisible for that reason. I was looking for approval from others. I had already started my people pleasing tendencies, finding my self-worth in what other people thought of me.

Most people pleasers wrestle with conflicting priorities. They believe that by focusing on others and staying in the background, they'll be liked because they're "nice" and don't draw attention to themselves. In fact, they figure everyone will notice how nice they are and will reach out to affirm them. But since they're in the background, nobody notices them—so they feel like they don't matter. They would rather have a "noninvisibility" cloak to make sure they're seen.

We feel invisible when we don't get the responses from others we want. We don't feel we're a vital part of the things going on around us. We're only seen for what we do, not who we are. We listen to other people for hours to make them feel cared about, hoping they'll ask about us at some point—but it never happens.

We feel like we don't matter. We're invisible.

## Blending In

There's good news and bad news about invisibility. The bad news is that it's usually something we've caused ourselves. The good news is that it's not that hard to fix.

A people pleaser often thinks, *People never notice me.* They assume it's because they're not worth noticing, so it becomes a marker of their value. They believe they're damaged and unlovable; if they were lovable, people would automatically pay attention to them.

When we intentionally try to put others first so they'll value us, we unintentionally slip off their radar. The very thing we're trying to do backfires and ensures we're not seen. We think it's because we're not worthy when it really means we're hiding. We've set ourselves up to be overlooked.

Here's the reality: most people aren't thinking about us anyway. They're thinking about themselves—just like we are.

This is especially noticeable during our teen years, when we're actively trying to determine who we are and what our place is in the world. Fitting in and being liked and accepted by others are a huge part of that process, and we're always gauging other people's reactions to see how we're doing. It consumes our focus and energy. When somebody likes us, we feel great. When they say something negative or just ignore us, we feel terrible.

What we didn't realize at the time was that everyone else was doing the same thing. If they liked us, it was because we made them feel good about themselves. If they were mean, it was because they had to put us down in order to feel superior.

Unfortunately, many people never grow out of that process. They're in their forties or fifties or sixties but still using others as mirrors to find their value. They don't realize that people still think primarily about themselves and don't pay much attention to them at all.

I once heard that everyone wears a sign around their neck that says, "Make me feel important today." I've spent my career working with everyone from corporate executives to assembly line workers and have found this to be true. Feeling important is a basic human need. When that need isn't satisfied, we feel invisible.

A good example is someone who joins a local church hoping to build caring relationships. They might select a large church where they can slip in and out of services unnoticed, but they don't engage in the small groups and activities that make up the life of the church. They wonder why no one is reaching out to them, not realizing they're waiting for others to make the first move. When it doesn't happen, their already fragile self-worth takes another blow.

## The Invisibility Cure

How do we fix this? That's the good news: *we can proactively do things to become noticeable.*

This doesn't mean an introvert has to become an extrovert to be noticed by others, or we have to pretend we're something we're not. It means we take measured actions in front of other people that exactly match who we are on the inside. We don't have to become loud and rude and obnoxious, like a used-car salesperson on late-night television. We just have to be ourselves, then do it in front of others.

Feeling invisible isn't something we wait for others to fix. It's something we fix by the choices we make.

Since most people are thinking of themselves more than they think of others, anything we do that makes them feel important puts us on their radar. We can't do it with false motives, just trying to get them to like us. That makes us a counterfeit, and they'll sense it almost immediately. It needs to be the result of a two-step process:

1. Learn to find your value internally rather than in the opinions of others. Build your inner confidence by finding truth in accurate "mirrors."
2. From that base of confidence, reach out to make others feel important by focusing on their needs. You'll be able to do it with pure motives since your security isn't dependent on their response.

When do you feel invisible?

Is it at social functions, when you feel like you're the most uncomfortable person in the room?

Is it when you express an opinion and other people discount what you say?

Is it when you're the youngest—or oldest—person in the room, and it feels like people see you as irrelevant?

Is it when you're seen only in your role ("the server"—"the salesperson"—"the barista") and not as a real person?

Is it when you're a parent and people see you as only an extension of your children?

Is it when you're in a routine, mundane stage of life, and you remember when your life was much more vibrant?

Seeing the circumstances where we feel invisible helps us decide what steps to take next. We can't expect others to change; it's up to us.

In the classic book *How to Win Friends and Influence People,* Dale Carnegie presents practical suggestions for growing interpersonal relationships. Even though it was written in 1936, the advice is still true today because it's based on what human beings want and need. If we accept the reality of those needs, we simply behave in ways that address those needs.

It's interesting that the book doesn't have a single suggestion about making others do things differently. It's all based on our ability to change what we do ourselves. As Viktor Frankl said in his book *Man's Search for Meaning,* "When we are no longer able to change a situation, we are challenged to change ourselves."[2]

So, what can we do to become more visible?

1. Take personal responsibility. Never blame anyone else for the way you feel. They're not responsible for your feelings;

you are. You might not like what someone says or does, but it's your choice how you respond to it.

2. Be objective. Don't get stuck in your own feelings. Instead, think of what you would tell a friend if they were in your situation and asked for your advice.

3. When you know you'll be in a social situation, plan your conversations ahead of time. Think through the people you could meet and craft some questions you could use to get things started. Someone told me once that if you work in a large company, you should always decide what you would say to your CEO if you ended up alone with him or her in an elevator. (For more on this, see my book *How to Communicate with Confidence*.)

4. In familiar relationships, do things differently. Family members and other friends who have known you for a long time are used to you relating in a certain way. They expect things to be the same as they were, so they have little reason to see you differently. If people know you're the one who always cooks and cleans at holiday gatherings, arrange to have the event at someone else's house this year—or go out to a restaurant together. Don't ask, just set it up and give people the details. If they complain, it's because you're not acting in the way they expect. They'll get over it.

5. Get out of your rut. For example, you might find yourself scrolling through social media and being consumed by the apparent success of others. Instead of dropping into comparison and discouragement, change your routines. Get up earlier. Take a different route to work or while running errands. Question everything you do to see if it's worth doing differently. As you make changes, you become a different person, and people will be more likely to notice the changes.

6. Trust your feelings. When you have a strong feeling, it's your body's way of trying to get your attention about something. Slow down and pay attention, then share those feelings with someone you trust. We often assume our feelings aren't that important so we stuff them down inside, staying in our heads and judging ourselves for having feelings. When that happens, it's common to numb those feelings with habits and ignore our needs instead of trusting those feelings and using them. Feelings are like the GPS of our life, so it's important to acknowledge them.

7. Engage simply with others. For example, I've often encountered frontline service people who seem cold and distant, like they would rather be anywhere else than waiting on me. It's easy to feel frustrated with them and grumble silently about the service. But I've found that simply making a warm connection with them through a few words can turn their whole attitude around. Their distance is because they see me as a customer (invisible) rather than a person, and they assume I'm doing the same with them. But when they feel valued, I've given them the opportunity for a few moments of a real relationship. Not only does it change the way I feel, but it changes the way they feel too.

What's one simple step you can take today to step out from under your invisibility cloak?

# 7

# I Need You to Affirm Me

## Fear of Inadequacy

When I use your ruler, I don't measure up.

Unknown

Why do we smile for pictures?

When somebody is taking our picture, they always say, "OK, smile for the camera!" Even if they don't, we usually do so instinctively. We know others are going to see the picture, so we want them to think positively about us. We smile whether we feel like it or not.

If a photographer said, "OK, just show what you're really feeling right now," what expression would you make?

Every year we get Christmas photos from our friends and family. Everybody's dressed perfectly and they're all smiling. But we know from personal experience they probably took five hundred shots to get one that looked like they liked each other.

Sometimes there's a letter attached that describes the highlights of their year. They usually talk about the great things each person has accomplished that year and how proud they are of them. They might mention challenges they've faced, but it's usually something they can't control (like an unexpected medical issue or a downsizing at work). I've never seen a paragraph in a Christmas letter like this:

> Terry turned nineteen in October. It's been tough for us to put up with him because he's so irresponsible (and he's still living at home). He got fired from his job for poor performance and spends most of his day on his phone. He's always late for everything, except for appointments with his parole officer. His girlfriend broke up with him shortly after he had her name tattooed on his arm (and it was misspelled). Our year felt like a train wreck because we don't know what to do with him. I guess that makes us bad parents too.

That one seems more honest, doesn't it? And in a strange way, kind of refreshing—because we can identify with imperfection.

We all seem to be positioning ourselves in our best light possible. Our résumés describe the great accomplishments we've had and the amazing abilities we can bring to a job. We want others to like us, so we emphasize the good stuff and leave off the bad stuff.

When you see a family photo, who do you look at first? That's right—yourself. You want to see how you look, because that's the way others will see you. If it's not flattering, you think it's a bad picture no matter how everyone else appears. You assume that when people see that picture, their eyes will be immediately drawn to how bad you look.

They're doing the same thing: looking at themselves. We're all comparing, thinking of ourselves and how we match up. So are they.

For a people pleaser, that's a recipe for disaster.

## Comparison: The Catalyst for Inadequacy

When everyone around us is showing only the positive side of life, it's easy to feel inadequate. We compare our reality with everyone else's public presentation and end up on the short side of the equation. That's the definition of inadequacy: *feeling like we're not good enough*.

You're having a productive day, and you're feeling pretty good about yourself. You're getting things done and feeling comfortable. Then you take a break to look at social media, and it puts you into a tailspin.

- People are posting all the amazing pictures of their family vacation and you think, *I wish we could afford that kind of vacation*.
- You see the "before/after" weight-loss pictures and realize you're perpetually on the "before" side.
- There's a sponsored post about having your kitchen remodeled. Now yours looks dated and drab.
- Someone who had a mundane life with financial challenges reports on the new business venture that brought them amazing success. If you join them, you can escape your mundane life too.

Deep inside, we realize that social media paints a picture that's crafted. But we still feel the impact. We see other people having a perfect life, and ours doesn't look nearly as good. Their kids get along well, their house looks like a model home, and everyone has plenty of time to relax and play board games. We think, *Well, my life is pretty mediocre compared to theirs*. The more we scroll, the more dissatisfied we become.

Before we went online, we felt fine. When we started comparing, we got depressed.

The worst part is that we assume what we see is accurate. We compare our real lives with their curated image. We see their image of wealth and happiness but really have no idea what they're thinking or feeling. We overlook our own successes and strengths by focusing on what they have and we don't.

Seriously, don't you get suspicious when you see pictures of a spotless family home? I've often wondered what kind of pictures we would see if a photographer simply knocked on that door unannounced and started taking pictures. My guess is that house would look a lot more like our houses do most of the time.

That doesn't mean the people we see on social media are dishonest. In most cases, they did lose the weight, build the business, find unexpected success, or go on that dream vacation. It's their personal journey, and they're excited about it and want to share their excitement.

But we're on our own journey, not theirs. The problem comes when we compare the challenges of our journey with the successes of their journey. We compare our insides with their outsides. Whenever we compare journeys in that way, we start feeling inadequate. We're "not enough."

It's even worse when others actively compare with us, putting us down in order to feel better about themselves. It might be direct or subtle, but it's hard to keep perspective when someone is personally attacking us. Sometimes it's a passive-aggressive family member or a sarcastic coworker who tries to triage us to the lowest position.

We used to visit an upscale neighborhood known for its annual Christmas light displays. People drove from miles away each year to experience the seasonal event where each homeowner tried to outdo their neighbors. Some houses had massive themed displays that covered the entire property, while others used cables and lights to connect their exhibits with neighbors across the street. Some homeowners did it themselves, while most hired professional firms to do the work. Dozens of homes participated, with very few exceptions.

We wondered about those exceptions. Were they not interested in decorating their houses, leaving dark spots in the neighborhood? Did they feel pressured by others in the neighborhood because they didn't participate?

It doesn't feel good to feel inadequate, and we want to fix it. That's when people pleasing can turn toxic. We become less real as we show others only our good side, hoping they'll be impressed with us. We're using them as a mirror of our value—and if they don't affirm us or notice us, our sense of worth goes down. That turns into a vicious cycle of increased people pleasing as we continually hope to feel better about ourselves.

Fortunately, there's a better way.

## Getting a New View

Comparison usually isn't something that takes years of therapy to overcome (though there might be deeper issues behind it that need to be explored). It usually involves two simple steps:

1. Recognize when we're focusing on others and comparing our journey with theirs.
2. Turn our focus back to our own journey and pay attention.

When we compare, we see someone as either above us or below us. In reality, we're just humans. Comparison is what separates us. Psychologists call our tendency to change our self-evaluation based on the feedback of others *contingent self-esteem*. It's dangerous because it's controlled by other people, and it requires living up to their standards to find our own value.

We weren't born feeling inadequate. It's something we learned, either by what we were told or what we observed. As kids, we didn't have enough life experience to determine if it was true or not. We just accepted it.

For example, if every time we failed at something we were told, "You can't do anything right!" we came to accept it. It became the filter through which we looked at the world. Since we believed we couldn't do anything right, we quit trying. That means we missed out on some amazing opportunities because of our fear of being proven inadequate. If not acknowledged, that fear carries into adulthood.

However, since we learned to feel inadequate, we also have the ability to unlearn it and can apply those two steps.

### 1. Recognize when you're comparing.

Think quickly: Who was the last person you compared yourself to? Was it while scrolling through social media or just during a live conversation with someone? How did you feel?

If comparison makes you feel inadequate, it's because you've given the control of your emotions to someone besides yourself. You're allowing them to determine your value instead of finding it in yourself. The other person might not even know it, because they're just living their life and you're watching and reacting. Pay attention to how you feel when you're comparing; you can use that feeling as a trigger. Catch yourself when that feeling surfaces, then ask yourself if it's because you're comparing yourself to someone else. When you recognize what's happening, it's easier to counteract the comparison instead of letting it control you.

You want strong relationships with mutual respect. When we compare ourselves with others, we're replacing companionship with comparison, and those relationships can't grow and develop. As author Kay Wyma said, "Contentment comes when we choose to see the immeasurable, incomparable beauty of each human, including the one in the mirror."[1]

### 2. Focus on your own journey.

The best way to stop comparing with others is to recognize your own uniqueness. You're the only "you" there is. You've cornered the market on being you, and nobody else can do it better.

If you're a turtle, it's frustrating if everyone is telling you to "soar like an eagle." It might look inviting, but it's not possible. The more you focus on what it would be like to be an eagle, the more energy you're diverting from becoming the best turtle you can be. Always be you, even if you don't think you're good enough or exciting enough. The more you can perfect being you, the more fulfillment you'll find in your own journey.

How do you overcome the negative image you've developed through a lifetime of comparison? By changing your mindset. Most people focus on overcoming the negatives in their life, which concentrates on fixing what's "wrong" with them. A healthier approach is to develop your areas of passion and uniqueness— focusing on the things that are "right."

I've heard several financial gurus say we should use 10 percent of our take-home income for personal development. If we do that, we're putting energy into things that help us grow and become better, not just fixing problems. The more we focus on the positive side of our lives, the less time or desire we'll have to compare with others.

Find your own unique abilities and build on them, creating a personal compass that gives you direction for your choices. That compass becomes your guide for living and frees you from the need for comparison.

Fear of inadequacy makes you focus on always "being better than others." When you look at the people around you, you're always having to move ahead of them to keep your self-worth intact.

Instead of being the best, try doing your best.

### The Right Way to Envy Others

So, how can you look at what others do without engaging in unhealthy comparison? Try these four steps:

### Avoid your triggers.

What usually triggers your need to compare and your feelings of inadequacy? Keep track of your triggers, and plan ways to intentionally avoid them.

- Too much social media? Remove those apps from your phone so they're not as accessible, or fast from social media on weekends.
- Listening to friends who brag about their accomplishments? Spend more time with people who are secure enough to just be your friends.
- Walking through a mall? Go with a friend so you're distracted and plan what you need instead of window shopping.
- Driving through an upscale neighborhood? Take a new route.

### Make a list.

Make a list of people you compare yourself with and how you feel when you do. Think through each one and note exactly what happens inside when you compare with them. Decide the best way to handle those moments before they occur. Monitor your negative beliefs and replace them with positive truth. Focus on your unique strengths and celebrate theirs without envy.

### Be grateful.

When you're triggered to compare, stop and consider what you already have. If you're driving through a neighborhood that's nicer than yours, remember that you don't know what's going on in that house. The outside only reflects what they have, not what their life is like. Gratefulness allows you to find contentment in your own present reality.

### Compare for positive change.

Instead of comparing with others around the lifestyle or posses-sions they seem to have, choose to align yourself with people you know who are generous, kind, or compassionate. Find someone who is an unusually good listener or seems to have an unhurried life and use that for motivation to become more like them. Invest your mental energy on people who inspire you, spending time with them if possible. Surround yourself with people you want to be like.

That's the key to overcoming the fear of inadequacy: pursuing adequacy in the right things.

# 8

# I Need You to Need Me

## Fear of Irrelevance

The way to gain a good reputation is to endeavor to be what
you desire to appear.

Socrates

Life is like climbing a mountain. You start at a city on one side of
the mountain, and you're headed for a city on the other side. Both
cities are the same distance from the mountaintop.

The first half of your life, you're climbing to the summit. It
takes great energy and focus, and everything you do is leading
you upward.

"Middle age" is when you reach the summit. It's a huge ac-
complishment, and the view is spectacular. You can look back
and see where you started, and you're amazed at how far you've
come. From the mountaintop, you can see the destination city in
the distance. It's just as far away as the place you started, but every
step brings it closer. It's also downhill, so it's an easier journey
and goes by a lot faster.

How old are you when that happens? Obviously, it depends on how long you live. Middle age is exactly that—the "middle" of the journey. Most people consider themselves "middle aged" when they're in their late forties or fifties. But running the numbers is revealing.

At the time of this writing (mid-2019), the average life expectancy in the United States is 78 years and 8 months. There are a lot of factors to consider, such as physical condition, genetics, and lifestyle choices. But if that's the average, it means most people reach the summit when they're just over thirty-nine years old.

We're either heading up or heading down.

Middle age tends to be a reflective time for most people. We review what we did in the first half of our journey and wonder if we've made a difference.

For a lot of people, that's a scary experience. If we feel like we squandered the first half of our life, there's often a sense of futility. *What difference am I making? Do I matter to anyone?* It's a common concern. Many people face their mortality and decide to change what they're doing so they make an impact. Others give up, assuming it's too late.

It's like the old *Far Side* cartoon by Gary Larson that shows a dog balancing on a high wire, riding a unicycle, spinning a hula hoop, and juggling above a circus audience. The caption reads, "High above the hushed crowd, Rex tried to remain focused. Still, he couldn't shake one nagging thought: He was an old dog and this was a new trick."

It's not just older people who struggle with growing irrelevance. Parents go through the first decade or so of parenting as the most significant people in their kids' lives. When those kids become teenagers, they begin the natural process of independence and separation. If we've found our identity in knowing that our kids need us, it's unnerving to see that role changing. Those kids need their parents just as much as before, but in a totally different way.

This is a tough one for people pleasers. When kids start expressing their own opinions and making their own decisions, some parents and grandparents don't feel as needed, and it's uncomfortable. We want to be liked by our kids, perhaps even wanting to be considered the "cool parents" by their friends. So we cut back on discipline or other things that cause our kids to get upset. We can end up making choices based on our own needs instead of doing what's best for our kids, trying to win back the admiration we've had for years.

When the kids leave and parents experience the "empty nest," it often results in an identity crisis. Suddenly, parents don't feel needed. They're not making a contribution anymore. They feel like they don't matter. *Who am I outside of my kids?* they may ask themselves.

Needing to "matter" is a basic human need, and we instinctively try to see if that need is being met. If it's not, we scramble to figure it out.

## Hardwired to Make a Difference

Everyone was created with a deep, inner compulsion to figure out what their purpose is in the world. That's why Rick Warren's book *The Purpose-Driven Life* became one of the bestselling books in history. The title spoke to a felt need that people have to do something more than just exist. If they don't figure it out, they can lead what Thoreau famously called "lives of quiet desperation"—living with an emptiness that comes with not feeling a sense of purpose.

We look at the people in our lives and think, *Do I matter to them? Am I making a difference in their lives? Are they better people because I'm in their lives?* If we can't tell, that sense of purpose goes undiscovered, and we keep searching. It's an itch that needs to be scratched, but no one is scratching it.

As people pleasers, we go back to the only thing we know: living for the opinions of others. We'll do whatever we can to make that person like us and affirm us. It's familiar territory and gives temporary relief. But since we're not contributing anything of real value, the response we get is empty because we realize we're not making a difference. We're just playing solitaire, getting quick wins occasionally that feel good in the moment, but they don't last.

People pleasing as a source of meaning is like eating junk food all day. It starts by satisfying us but quickly wears off. Because it's taking away our "felt need" (hunger), we lose our appetite for making a real contribution.

The biggest contribution we can make in the world isn't being popular. It's becoming 100 percent ourselves. It's the only thing we can contribute that is totally unique, and it's impossible for anyone else in the world to contribute in the same way.

In other words, your uniqueness is your number-one tool for making a massive difference in the world and in the lives of the people in your personal sphere of influence. After all, if everyone was the same, how could any change happen?

If you want to make a difference, *be different.*

## Look Outward, Not Inward

People pleasers do a lot of things for others, but we're always looking at ourselves while we're doing them. Outwardly, we appear to be compassionate and generous—which is exactly how we want others to see us. But our motive makes it backfire.

It's OK to please others and meet their needs if the true motive is the good of those other persons. But if our generosity comes solely from a place of personal need (we give just to feel better about ourselves), it leads to discouragement and depression. Our deep, inner need to make a difference doesn't go away; it gets louder.

When we're feeling useless and wallowing in self-pity, our sense of value seems to spiral downward. How can we reverse the spiral? It may sound counterintuitive, but it's by reaching out to others.

It doesn't solve the problem immediately, but when we're focused on helping others, we're not able to focus as much on ourselves. Just as a person can't run in two directions at the same time, we can't give our full attention to both ourselves and others. When we're thinking about meeting another person's needs, it keeps us from thinking about our own misery.

"Wait—haven't you been saying that focusing on others is the problem for a people pleaser? And we need to work on ourselves first?"

Yes, but it's our *motive* that's important. Unhealthy people pleasers focus on others in order to win their approval. Healthy people pleasers do it to genuinely meet the needs of others. Anytime a healthy person struggles with a lack of purpose, reaching outward is the quickest way to regain the proper perspective.

Research such as that done by Dr. Susan Noonan has shown that when people do active volunteer work, it almost always elevates their mood.[1] Why? Because they're making a difference.

- They feel needed.
- Their self-confidence grows, along with their sense of purpose.
- They're making a tangible contribution.
- They learn new skills, which opens new opportunities.
- They get distracted from their own negative thoughts.
- They usually dress up a bit, which helps with self-respect.
- They develop social skills.

If someone feels like they have nothing of value to offer, seeing tangible results in the lives of others can provide the motivation to keep going. People who are depressed are often low in energy, and it's tough to get started doing anything—which drives the depression even deeper. Volunteering provides a reason to push through and get out the door, and that alone can often lift someone's mood.

When you're feeling bad about yourself because you think you don't matter to anyone, you're probably waiting for others to come and affirm you. That can be an exercise in futility, because most people aren't thinking about you. Take the initiative to reach out, and you'll provide them a chance to respond. Even if they don't, you'll still feel better about you.

## A Strategy for Sharing

Everyone struggles with a sense of irrelevance from time to time as they progress through different seasons of life. It's normal, and it's something that takes time to process.

This is especially tough for a people pleaser, because your self-worth is at stake. Once you convince yourself that you're becoming irrelevant, it's easy to feel like you don't matter. The wisdom you've gained throughout your life just doesn't seem to fit anymore.

But your unique wisdom is never irrelevant or out of style. Maybe the packaging could be updated, but what you have to offer is always a source of great value to others.

I've spent most of my career in front of a classroom, in both a university setting and corporate conference rooms. Most of that time I have been able to connect easily with seminar participants and engage them quickly. But thirty years and three thousand seminars in, I hit a place where it felt like it was taking longer and longer for that engagement to happen. The audiences were looking younger, and my hair was getting "lighter." I felt like they saw me and thought, *Who's the old guy? We have to spend the whole day listening to him? How can he be relevant?* Once we started it didn't take long to connect, but I felt like I had to prove myself and convince them I had something valuable to contribute.

One day I mentioned that to a colleague who happened to be sitting in on one of my sessions. She was surprised I was feeling that way, and said, "No, I think it's just the opposite. They know you're older than them, but they're not dismissing you. They're assuming you're like the wise college professor they had who knows a lot, and they're looking forward to what you have to say. They're not expecting you to be one of them; they're looking for you to be you so they can learn something from what you have to offer."

That was a major paradigm shift for me. I had been feeling irrelevant, but it was all in my mind. It wasn't real; it was my assumption. Once I changed my perspective, my confidence in front of any audience was completely restored.

Fear of irrelevance is self-imposed. When we think we're winding down, we might actually be ramping up. When we feel like we don't matter, that can be the trigger to double down on making a difference.

What does that journey back to relevance look like? Consider these perspectives.

### Do work that helps others, but don't worry about the outcome.

Serve others without measuring what impact it's having on them. Most people aren't committed to giving us a positive response, even if they're receiving great benefit. Just do the work.

### Become curious.

When we're feeling irrelevant, it's easy to stop learning or growing. We think, *Why do I need to grow? Nobody's listening anyway.* But the more we grow, the more we have to offer others.

### Pick your focus.

It's easy to get excited about a ton of different things, but we have to be selective. Narrow the field and decide where you're going to put your energy. Others might not like it when you don't join them in their passion, but don't be intimidated. Pick a lane and stay in it. Even Gandhi didn't do everything; he just believed he could make a difference and focused there.

*Build your expertise.*

Once you've picked your area of focus, keep learning. Read extensively, take courses, and spend time with people in that field. Your life experience added to growth will ensure your relevance in that field.

## The Gift of Relevance

Everyone wants to matter. People pleasers have simply chosen an inappropriate way of meeting that need, and it produces the exact opposite over time.

Making a difference comes from making a choice. Fear of irrelevance can be replaced by being real, being unique, and being compassionate.

It's time to start down a new path!

# PART 3

# BUILDING BLOCKS FOR WORLD-CLASS PEOPLE PLEASING

When we moved into our current house a few years ago, it had a large wooden deck attached to the back of the house that was perfect for our needs, extending to the back fence and wrapping around the house.

However, the bad news was that all its boards were rotting. Over years of exposure, those surface boards had become warped and full of splinters, and the nails holding them down had pulled out. We painted it and replaced the loose nails several times, trying to make it look as good as possible. We just wanted to hide the way it looked so people wouldn't notice the shape it was in.

We lived with it for a few years, but it got progressively worse. We couldn't walk barefoot because of the loose nails, and in a number of places we felt we'd fall through at any moment. The more the deck rotted, the harder it was to maintain the image. It became more and more obvious what its real condition was.

We saved up until we had enough money to replace those boards and started pulling them up. We figured that new deck boards would solve the problem. What we didn't consider was that the structural framework holding it all up was also starting to decay. It wasn't as bad as the surface, but we knew we needed to replace it too. It might hold things up for a while, but over time the decay would compromise the entire structure.

Fixing that deck properly took a lot longer than planned and cost a lot more than expected. But we knew we couldn't just cover it up and pretend everything was OK. We had to put in the effort to do it right. As a result, the deck became both solid and good-looking.

People pleasing is like that too. In the beginning, we try to clean up what we're feeling, hiding it from others and pretending to be OK so people will be impressed. We might even replace the boards so we look brand-new.

But there's decay happening below the surface. We know it, but we've kept it hidden for years. As time goes on, it gets worse, and it's harder to hide. We're afraid to peek below the surface because we know things aren't right. We're afraid of what we might find.

------

In the last five chapters, we've crawled under the deck and looked around. We've taken an honest look at the five things we need the most and what we're most afraid of. When we look closely at those fears and talk through options for dealing with them, they don't look nearly as scary as before. That's our current foundation.

Now, it's time to rebuild. With a clear understanding of the job to be done, we can purchase supplies and tools and start the process. It's not something that will be done overnight, but we can take the first step. Then the next. Then the next.

What are the key things we need to acquire in order to rebuild? Here are ten building blocks where we'll put our energy. They're not in any particular order, so you can choose where to begin. Read through them all and decide which have the most value in your situation. Then pick one and start building.

1. Being proactive—*take personal responsibility.*
2. Staying connected—*access the value of relationships.*
3. Building confidence—*see yourself accurately.*
4. Crafting integrity—*live an honest life.*
5. Strengthening communication—*master the tools of connection.*
6. Fostering curiosity—*maintain a thirst for wonder.*
7. Sharpening focus—*pay attention without distraction.*
8. Practicing self-care—*invest in yourself.*
9. Developing gratefulness—*search for the positive.*
10. Keeping perspective—*accept reality.*

None of these are difficult by themselves, and they're easy to implement if we take small steps. Once these building blocks are in place, they allow us to use our people pleasing in the healthiest possible way, impacting the lives of others around us. That's the focus of this next section: building a simple strategy to change our lives.

# 9

# Building Block #1— Being Proactive

## Take Personal Responsibility

Never forget that only dead fish swim with the stream.

Malcolm Muggeridge[1]

She didn't fit the typical coffee shop crowd.

Usually, the place was filled with students with computers, business people with lattes, and a few older folks scanning their iPads. But not this woman. Her silver hair was styled comfortably. She also had a sense of fashion without being presumptuous. She was *stylin'*. She and a much younger woman sat across from each other a few feet down from me, and there was a small, open box between them.

The box on the table had a familiar logo: *Apple*.

When the older woman spoke, she sounded confident, but not in a pushy way. "I can do this, you know. That's why I bought it."

"Absolutely, Grandma," the younger woman replied. "You've never been afraid to try new stuff."

"Maybe that'll happen when I get old," she said.

"So, how old *are* you now?"

"I'm only ninety. Now, show me what else this thing can do."

The granddaughter, a woman who appeared to be in her early forties, let her grandma hold the device herself and try things out while she talked her through the steps.

I was there to work on an article I was writing and clean up some emails. But this was too good to ignore. A ninety-year-old woman had just purchased an Apple watch and was committed to learning how to use it.

"Will it show my heart rate?" I heard her ask.

"It sure will, Grandma. See? It's right here."

"That's important," the woman said. "I'll check it every morning. If it shows I have a pulse, I'll get up." They both laughed.

"Does it keep track of how many steps I take?"

"Yep. And it also shows exactly where you are, and I can see it on a map on my computer."

"That's good. I'm supposed to walk ten thousand steps a day. If I get lost, I'll just keep walking until you come find me." They both laughed again.

This went on for another thirty minutes. Grandma tried each instruction several times until she got it and could move on to the next. The younger woman didn't show any irritation when it took multiple tries. Her patience gave her grandma a gift of great respect.

Finally, it was time for them to go. The stylin' grandma wrapped the watch around her wrist and snugged it up.

"Thanks, honey," she said to her granddaughter. "Next time, can you show me how it connects with my phone?"

And they left.

I watched them walk slowly away and realized this wasn't one of those older marathon runners still in peak physical shape. She was a physically elderly woman who decided not to *think* elderly.

She had a young attitude because she took responsibility for herself.

She was *proactive*.

## Taking Control of Your Choices

People pleasers base their sense of value on the opinions and reactions of others. They see themselves as a sculpture, and often allow other people to hold the chisel (or they *think* another person holds the chisel). They have become victims because they let their lives be shaped by what they think others are thinking. They feel powerless, but they never let others know. They're hostage to their imagined notions of others' thoughts. It's too risky to trust others with the truth about themselves, so they constantly manage their image.

When that happens, they sabotage their unique contribution. They might take initiative to try something new, but they're immediately watching how others respond. If they feel the slightest criticism, they give up. It could have been something energizing, but they'll never know. They allow their choices to be determined by what others want, not what they themselves want.

The first building block toward recovery is to be proactive: taking responsibility for your own life. That means you never blame anyone else for your circumstances, and you always make choices based on your own unique perspective.

Dr. Steven Covey, author of *The 7 Habits of Highly Effective People*, often said, "I am not a product of my circumstances; I am a product of my decisions." Being proactive is recognizing that it's futile to blame anyone else for where you are in your life. Others might pressure you to react to something, but you always have the freedom to choose your response. You control your choices, and your choices control your destiny.

"But what about things that are out of my control? I can't control the economy or the hurtful actions of other people. They've messed up my life, and there's nothing I can do about it," you may say. While we can't control what others do, we can control how we respond to their actions. When we are controlled by bitterness and anger over what others do, we give away our freedom to choose. We've given that person control of our emotions—and that's not the kind of person we want controlling our lives.

Being proactive doesn't minimize the hurt caused by others. It just means we choose not to be enslaved by them. We look at the past realistically, then decide how to move forward. In other words, we keep the keys to our happiness in our own pockets.

As Reinhold Niebuhr wrote in the classic serenity prayer:

> God, grant me the serenity to accept the things I cannot
>   change,
> Courage to change the things I can,
> And wisdom to know the difference.[2]

Proactive people learn to live a life with no regrets, which is the foundation for recovering from a lifelong pattern of people pleasing.

## Living without Regret

Regret usually centers on things *we've* done, not what *others* have done. Another person might make a choice that puts our lives in a tailspin, and we feel hurt or anger—but not regret.

When we view ourselves through the lens of regret, it's never positive and it's almost always overblown. We regret *something we did*, but we often turn that into regret for *who we are*. It's personal. We feel shame and guilt because of something we did, but if we can't deal with it, we lose our value. "I did something bad" becomes "I *am* bad."

That's a dangerous place to live. When we hang on to "if only," we're stuck in the past—and it sabotages our future.

Most regret fits into one of two categories: things done in ignorance, or things done by intention.

### Ignorance

I had surgery last week for skin cancer. It's not the first time—in fact, I've been making payments on my dermatologist's Mercedes for years. He said that some people have skin that's just more prone to it than other people, and I'm one of the lucky ones.

Growing up in Arizona in the sixties didn't help. Nobody used sunscreen back then. In fact, we would use things like baby oil to magnify the sun's impact. I'm feeling the consequences now. But I didn't know any better at the time.

That's ignorance.

### Intention

When I was a teenager, I remember hearing about compound interest. If I could find a way to save two thousand dollars per year between the ages of sixteen and twenty-two (and invest it at a realistic rate of return), I'd never have to save anything else after age twenty-two to have a million dollars at retirement.

I did more research and found similar models. I knew what to do, but I chose not to do it. If I had, I'd be in a whole different place financially than I am now.

Common choices that lead to regret include things like:

- Who we dated in college
- Job choices
- Moving away from family for a job
- Not moving toward an opportunity because of fear
- Getting a cat
- Forming harmful habits
- Tattoos that represent values or relationships that have changed

"Intentional regret" is tougher than "ignorance regret" because we knew better but did it (or didn't do it) anyway.

When the stakes are higher, it's even tougher. It's one thing to buy a used car that wasn't the best choice and is now falling apart. It's another to have broken relationships because of things you said or did in the past. If you break trust with someone, it doesn't reappear with a simple "I'm sorry." Trust takes time to rebuild.

My wife and I know what we did wrong in our parenting when our kids were growing up. They didn't come with instructions, so we tried to figure it out. We've apologized for the mistakes, but they'll always feel the impact of our choices.

If you're living in the past because of regret, it's not really the past. It's the present, because that's where you are today—*and it closes the door to your future.*

Freedom from people pleasing comes from living in the present. It's proactively choosing to remember the past accurately but keeping it in the past. No matter how we've previously operated, we're not condemned to living there in the future. We can always make new choices and move in new directions.

## How to Get Unstuck

What would it feel like if you could live free from regret? How would your relationships and conversations be different? How would you feel about the future? Would you have hope?

The past is real, so we can't ignore it. If we ignore it, it stays alive inside us and becomes a cancerous growth in our journey. We need to face it, then take control of it.

*You are not your past.* Your choices in the present determine your future. Proactive people learn from the past but don't live there. They take responsibility for it and build on it, but they're not defined by it.

Today is a new day. Today, you can start moving away from regret. Recognize you can't change what's happened in the past.

It's history. Regret comes when you can't forgive yourself and give up trying.

Pick one of your regrets and challenge it. Since the past doesn't change, what single step could you take now to move back into control?

- If you didn't handle your money wisely, you could read a book on how to take control of your finances in the future.
- If you didn't exercise growing up, you could find two accountability partners and begin a fitness journey together.
- If you got into a career you've never liked, you can enroll in an online course to gain skills to take you in a new direction.

If your car runs out of gas on the way to a job interview, you'll feel regret for not filling up earlier—especially if you miss the job opportunity. It's easy to beat yourself up when that happens. It's important to face those feelings and admit them to yourself, and maybe to others too. But it's futile to stay on the side of the road thinking, *I'm so stupid. I just ruined everything. I always do that.* Rephrase that thought into something more accurate: *I made a bad choice. I'm OK—but I messed up. I'll move forward.* Then call a tow truck.

Always take the next right step. The more you begin moving forward, the less grip the past will have on you. Regret isn't a given; you can start releasing it today.

Be intentional about taking responsibility for everything you do. Admit the mistakes, embrace the successes, and make a new pattern for your life. When you catch yourself living for the opinions of others, use it as a trigger to choose differently. Ask yourself, *What choice would I make if I wasn't worried about what others would think?* Then make that choice, no matter what they might *really* say.

In many cases, being proactive means learning to say no. It's a lot more comfortable to say yes, and it might seem insignificant. But those little things add up. You have only so much time available to you. Every time you say yes, you're saying no to everything else. When you're overwhelmed and exhausted, doing more isn't the answer; doing less is.

For a people pleaser, saying no seems almost impossible. But with a little careful thought and planning, it's just a matter of crafting your response ahead of time. When just saying a flat no feels rude, try something like this: "That sounds great—what a neat opportunity! I wish there was more time in the day. But if I say yes to this, I'm saying no to something I've already committed to that's right in line with where I'm headed. But thanks for asking—I'm really grateful you considered me!"

It's your life, not theirs. Replace blame with personal responsibility, and it becomes the foundation for everything you do in the future.

That's where you start, and it can happen today.

# 10

# Building Block #2—
# Staying Connected

## Access the Value of Relationships

If you want to go quickly, go alone. If you want to go far,
go together.

African Proverb

"Welcome to our hotel," the desk clerk said. I've heard those words
thousands of times over the years. Most of the time, they're spoken by a smiling employee who wants my first encounter with the
hotel to be positive.

"We have your payment information on file . . . breakfast starts
at six . . . would you like a wake-up call?" It's a routine conversation, but pleasant. Like the safety instructions given by a flight
attendant, it's easy to glaze over the content. In some form, I've
heard it all before.

Until this time. "We do have one little problem, sir."

"What's that?" I asked, surprised by the change in the usual script.

"The key readers aren't working. It'll take a couple of days to get them fixed."

That didn't sound good. "So, what are you saying?"

"You can't get in your room," he replied, and I looked around for the hidden cameras, wondering which candid show I'd be appearing on. "I'm really sorry," he continued. "But every time you want to go into your room, just come to the front desk. We'll walk down there with you and open the door with our master key." He asked someone to cover for him at the desk, then stepped out to accompany me through the corridors. My room was at the far end of the hotel, so my new companion and I had time to talk along the way.

"Have you had many angry guests because of this?" I asked.

"Not angry, but a little frustrated. They know these things just happen, but it makes it inconvenient for them."

"Don't you get tired of walking with people over and over again?" I continued.

"Nope," he said. "But it has surprised me."

"How so?"

"I always thought I was interacting with a lot of people every day. But really, I was just having the same conversation over and over with different people. Now, I have time to get to know them a little. They're like, well, *real people*."

I chuckled to myself, thinking about how often "good customer service" might be focusing on the wrong thing: *appearing* to care instead of *caring*.

He went on. "With just that short conversation, it's like we've connected. We know each other, just a little. It's changing the way I look at my job. I'm supposed to make people feel welcome, but it's not real. I'm just smiling and saying the right words. But when I have a real conversation that goes beyond that greeting, they *actually* feel welcome."

They become real people.

## The Value of Connection

That was last week, and I've thought about that conversation a lot in the past few days. As a recovering people pleaser, I wonder how many quick, casual chats I've had that are cordial . . . but I'm just going through the motions of caring. I have some key phrases that get a predictable response, so I use them frequently. My real concern has often been to impress the other person, not to value them.

We can't have long, deep encounters with everyone who crosses our path. But what if we saw each person we encounter as a "real" person? That doesn't mean our conversation has to be any longer. It just means that I'll see the desk clerk, the grocery cashier, or the person behind me in line as human. If I do that, I won't try to force conversation or manipulate it or even avoid it. I'll just *see them* as a unique person, going through unique stuff on their unique journey. I'll be reminded that I'm on my unique journey as well—and both of us are OK.

I'll see them through a different lens. When I see them as "real," the words aren't as important. I just have to care. It shifts my momentary focus from "all about me" to "all about them."

## Do I Really Need Other People?

"OK, I know where you're headed with all this," a people pleaser says. "You're going to say that community is important, and it helps us grow and accomplish more than we could on our own. I get that. But I already spend most of my time in the presence of other people, trying to get them to like me and respond the way I need them to. It's exhausting. I need fewer people in my life, not more."

There's some truth in that. People pleasers are usually highly attuned to other people, and they know how much they need those people. But the problem is their motive. People pleasers need others to affirm them so they feel valued. They're involved in community—sort of—but it's one-sided. They're in it for their own benefit, not mutual benefit.

That approach is deceptive, because they're totally focused on others. But that's only on the surface. Healthy people know their need for community, but it's so they can do life together. When two people stop trying to impress each other and simply share the journey, they both become better for it.

People pleasers are probably the biggest purchasers of self-help books. They don't like the way their life feels, and they want to grow and improve. But it's tough for them to reach out to others when they depend on those people for affirmation, so the only option is to try to grow on their own. That makes them feel even more frustrated over time, because real growth happens in community, not in isolation. Without challenging input from others, it's easy to believe our own thoughts are accurate—which means they don't need to be changed.

## Mutual Mentoring

When people pleasers do reach out, they're often looking for a mentor—someone who is an expert able to impart the knowledge they need to grow and move forward. They assume that getting the right mentor will help them learn the skills of life, and everything will be OK.

There's real value in mentoring, where you intentionally hang out with someone who's further along the path than you. I've been on both the "mentor" side and the "mentee" side, and it's been priceless. But I've also seen one-sided mentoring relationships where the mentor is expected to give while the mentee expects to receive. The mentoring flows only downward, and it becomes more of a transaction than a relationship.

But that's not how real life works. One-way relationships aren't real, and they don't last.

Mentoring doesn't just take place from older to younger, from wiser to less experienced, from successful to start-up. It takes place anytime two people come together in a real relationship and have the humility to learn from each other. We've all had experiences another person hasn't had. When we just listen to each other, we become different people. It's not a formal structure; it's organic. It happens because we care.

I'm not against formal mentoring at all. But if that's the only way we define it, we lose some priceless opportunities to impact others and be impacted by them. The purpose of a mentoring relationship is to "get better" and grow. Having (or being) a formal mentor is one way to do that. But in addition, there are three other people we need to have in our lives:

- Someone we can *follow*—someone (often older) who's further ahead on the path.
- Someone we can *walk with*—a friend who's in the same life stage we are.
- Someone we can *lead*—someone (often younger) who's further back on the path.

This revises the idea of mentoring from just being one person pouring into another person to involving traveling as companions and changing because we're doing it together.

What if we intentionally connected with others at different stages on the journey and walked with them? Maybe we'd all grow exponentially.

## The Upside of Community

Things happen in real relationships that don't happen when we're alone. If we're doing life by ourselves, it's easy to focus on everything negative about ourselves as we compare with the positive things in others. We lose perspective of what's real and true as our thinking spirals downward. When life gets tough, we have to face it with only the resources we already have instead of sharing others' resources.

How do you feel when you've been around someone who is completely present when you're broken, listens to you without trying to fix you, and speaks the truth without judgment? These are the people who give us life, who reach inside and hold our hearts when we're hurting. We experience their forgiveness and grace when we can't forgive ourselves.

Have you ever tried to heal your heart by yourself? It's depressing. In fact, I heard a psychologist say one time that depression is the only emotion we can't pull ourselves out of. By definition, we're in a pit we can't escape without the help of another.

Simply stated, we're created for community.

How many people do we need in our lives? Not as many as we might think. People pleasers want everyone to like them, so they're performing for the masses. This causes them to believe that the more people who like them, the better.

But we're talking about genuine relationships, not glowing fans. It's better to have a few deep relationships than hundreds of admirers. We begin with one person who's real and allows us to be exactly who we are. They're safe, and they're not trying to change us. They just let us be ourselves, and we go through the journey together.

I asked someone once, "How many friends does it take to make you happy?" They replied, "One more."

There was actually some research done a few years back at Cornell University that describes how the process works. Dr. Robin Dunbar did some intricate studies and found that the number of friends we need relates to the size of a section of the brain called the *neocortex*, which processes such things.

It turns out most of us can be in relationship with about 150 people.[1] That doesn't mean "best friends" but rather people we recognize, interact with occasionally, and have some connection with.

We'll have different levels of interaction with them, of course. A few will reach "best friend" status while others will be regular contacts, extended family members, work colleagues, or people we do business with. For example, we might have a conversation with our doctor a few times a year but we speak with our spouse multiple times each day.

Dunbar suggests that most people find happiness with three to five *best friends*, one of these being a *very best friend*. There's a bigger circle after that, with thirty to fifty *good friends*—and everybody else makes up the rest of our relationships. Anyone outside of that group of 150 will be pretty much off our radar.

It's like having a whole bunch of sweaters in your closet, but you end up wearing only five or six most of the time.

Even Jesus had a group of only seventy people considered part of his "tribe." Of those, there were twelve he did life with, three of those twelve were his close friends, and one of those three was his closest friend.

Maybe we could learn something from that.

## One Final Reason

When I was a kid, our annual family vacation was usually at Sequoia National Park in central California. We would rent a "housekeeping cabin" where we'd cook on a woodstove, then put the leftover food scraps in metal trash cans on the canvas-covered porch.

Shortly after dusk each night, we would watch through the windows as black bears would rummage through those trash cans, only three feet from us. (No, they don't let you intentionally attract bears anymore.)

During the day, we would visit the general store, take day hikes out to Crescent Meadow, and climb Morro Rock. We would hold peanuts on our laps and watch the chipmunks climb up our legs to grab them, and we'd watch blue jays fight for the ones that dropped (the peanuts, not the chipmunks).

My favorite adventure was the nature walks led by the park rangers. Every day we would go on a different excursion where these experts described the intricate details of our surroundings. One day it would be about trees. The next it would be about animals. Then we would learn about the conditions on the forest floor that enabled seeds to grow.

Even at a young age, I was fascinated. I remember how I felt when a ranger said, "We're surrounded by the largest and oldest living things in the world, the giant Sequoia Redwoods." She told us that when the first European explorers stepped onto the shore of the New World, these trees had already been alive for over a thousand years.

General Sherman was the granddaddy of them all. By volume, it's the biggest tree in the world. Other trees are taller, but General Sherman is the beefiest. Weighing about two million pounds, it's been around for about 2,200 years (which means it was already two hundred years old when Christ was born). Our whole group would circle the tree and touch fingertips, but we never had enough people to reach around its trunk.

"What do you think keeps this tree from falling over?" the ranger asked. I had paid attention in science class and remembered what my teacher told me. "The taproot," I said. "Trees have one huge root going straight down that holds it in place." I was proud of my chance to show how smart I was.

"Good guess," she said, "but these giant Sequoias don't have taproots."

Now I was confused. I thought taproots were the only thing that kept trees from falling over during storms, earthquakes, and other natural events. Now this ranger was telling us that the largest trees in the world were missing their taproots. So, what held them up?

"These trees have surface roots that extend sideways for a huge distance—often covering a whole acre of ground from a single tree," she said. "But that's still not enough to hold them up. These trees grow in groves, close to other trees. Their roots reach out and intertwine with the roots of every other tree. That's where the strength comes from. In simple terms, *the trees hold each other up* during the worst conditions. If one of these trees was alone, it wouldn't survive."

We value independence. I know I do; it's hard for me to ask for help or depend on someone else. I can be like a two-year-old telling my mom, "I can do it all by myself."

But we aren't made for independence. We're made for *interdependence*.

We don't realize that we need each other until the storm hits. That's when we discover we don't have taproots. If we're all alone, we can't stand up to the pressure. The ability to handle life well doesn't happen when we're isolated; it happens when we're interconnected.

We're made to hold hands through life.

# 11

# Building Block #3— Building Confidence

## *See Yourself Accurately*

The secrecy of my job does not allow me to know what I'm doing.

Anonymous Pentagon worker

Most hotel rooms have printed instructions on how to handle natural disasters. In California, I've read what to do if there's an earthquake. In Oklahoma, I've seen instructions on responding to a tornado. In some coastal states, I've prepared for a hurricane.

In Fairbanks, Alaska, I learned what to do in case of moose.

I was amused when I saw the sheet on the desk in the rustic-themed room at the lodge where I had come to train the hotel employees. *Clever*, I thought. *They wrote this up to sound like the ones in other hotels.* I assumed it was just a joke, because moose seemed pretty harmless when the only one I'd ever known was one on TV named Bullwinkle.

I walked the paper down to the front desk. "What's this about?" I asked.

The desk clerk looked at me as if I was from another planet. "It's about what to do if you meet a moose. Just like it says."

"So, do you get many of them around here?" I was expecting a chuckle or two as we shared the joke.

"Every couple of days," she replied without expression.

"Really?"

"Really. They wander around the parking lot out here. That's why we have the low doorframe at the entrance. Once in a while, they try to come inside."

"Is it a problem if you run into one?" I asked.

"Could be. If they decide they don't like you, they can do some real damage."

"So, what are you supposed to do if you meet one in the parking lot?"

After a brief, condescending stare, she pointed back to the paper I was holding. "Read that," she said. "That's why we put it in the room." I was a little embarrassed, but now I was curious. I looked down at the simple instructions: *If you encounter a moose, stand behind a tree.*

"Are you serious?" I asked.

"Yep. You don't want to run away, because they'll catch you. But if you stand behind a tree, it's hard for them to get around it with those big antlers. Pretty soon they'll get tired of trying and wander off."

It didn't seem very noble to imagine my obituary reading, "Killed by a moose," so I decided to follow her instructions.

I went for a long, frigid walk that day. The scenery was great, but it was hard to relax. I was always looking for the nearest tree, just in case I caught the interest of something large and brown. I didn't see any moose that day—which was a little disappointing, since I was so well prepared. And I haven't been able to use my newfound moose knowledge in Southern California.

I did learn three other valuable lessons that day:

1. I don't know everything.
2. Assuming I know everything can get me in trouble.
3. It's good to listen to people who know what I don't.

Those are foreign lessons for a people pleaser. Since they need others to admire them, they have to appear to be competent and have all the answers. If they admit they don't know something, they might be seen as incompetent. So they make sure others see them as wise but humble at the same time. It's all part of the image.

Humility isn't weakness; true humility comes when a person has true confidence. If that person is only pretending to be confident, it comes across as arrogance.

## The Value of Confidence

How do people perceive you? Do they see you as confident and in control or arrogant and cocky?

Confidence is inspiring. We're drawn to confident people. Being around them makes us feel better about ourselves. They give us hope we can grow. We think, *I want to be as confident as they are.* Arrogance is irritating. We're turned off by people with an arrogant attitude. They make an effort to show how much they know, and they always have to be right. We think, *Who do they think they are, anyway?*

It might seem to us like confidence and arrogance are identical, and it's true there's a fine line between the two. We think arrogance is "too much" confidence, and we don't want to be seen as arrogant. Even if we feel confident, we assume we'll be seen as arrogant if we talk about it too much—so we stay quiet.

But the two terms really have nothing to do with each other.

116

Confidence is about having security in the truth of who you are. It means you don't have to pretend to be something you're not. It means seeing yourself accurately and accepting it. You don't feel the need to prove yourself to others, and you're willing to learn from them.

Arrogance often comes from a *lack* of confidence. When a person feels insecure, they don't want anyone to know it. So they overcompensate by acting confident. It's an attempt to convince others of something that isn't true. If they were truly confident, they wouldn't need the approval of others.

Confident people aren't usually arrogant. Arrogant people aren't usually confident.

People pleasers *pretend* to be confident. If, instead, they can learn to *be* confident, they'll become the best kind of people pleaser—the kind that makes a serious impact in the lives of others.

## Spotting Confidence versus Arrogance

There are subtle cues in people's behavior that cause us to accurately categorize them as confident or arrogant. The more cues there are, the easier it is to determine their perspective.

### Respect

Arrogant people are concerned about themselves more than others, so they frequently interrupt others to present their own ideas. Confident people genuinely want to hear others' perspectives. They're not threatened by disagreement and can allow a difference of opinion without feeling the need to correct the other person.

### Punctuality

Arrogant people are often habitually later than is socially acceptable, and they don't apologize when it happens. If a confident person is going to be late, they call ahead to let the other person know and apologize for the delay. They realize the other person is just as busy as they are, so they make sure they're not wasting their time.

### Listening

Arrogant people listen to others only so they can come up with a good response. Confident people listen for understanding and aren't afraid to say, "That's an interesting position. Tell me more," without having to inject their own perspective.

### Name-dropping

Arrogant people resort to name-dropping to impress others. It's "fame by association." Confident people might know someone famous but don't need to throw it around. In the right context, they'll share the relationship as appropriate, but only to inform, not to impress.

### Body language

Arrogant people often reflect their arrogance in their posture, with an exaggerated swagger when they enter a room. Confident people reflect a solid, comfortable posture when they're with others. They're not trying to capture attention, but true confidence simply attracts others through its presence.

### Blame

Arrogant people never admit mistakes or being wrong, and they blame others for anything negative. Confident people are proactive, taking responsibility for their choices and responses. They're the first to say, "I was wrong. I'm sorry."

### Positioning

Arrogant people have to "one-up" everyone else who shares an experience. Confident people enjoy the stories and ask to hear more.

Take an honest look at yourself in each of these categories. How do you measure up? Based on that criteria, would people who know you well say you lean toward confidence or arrogance?

## Trying It Out

A close friend of mine was following the advice in Dr. Henry Cloud's book *How to Get a Date Worth Keeping*, where he suggests taking a nonserious dating approach with a number of people to learn what you like and what you don't (instead of looking for the one right person). She was challenged to go on dates with at least twenty-five different guys, never repeating companions until all twenty-five dates were completed.

She told me most of those guys spent the entire date trying to demonstrate how successful and deserving they were, and why she should be impressed with them. One even picked her up in a helicopter and whisked her off to dinner. When he found out there wouldn't immediately be a second date, he was incensed she wasn't thrilled with him.

He wasn't confident; he was arrogant.

Most of the twenty-five men were the same way, except for number eight. He was quietly confident and didn't feel the need to prove himself.

She married number eight about six years ago, and it's been amazing.

## The Key to Confidence

Author Marianne Williamson said, "Your playing small does not serve the world. There is nothing enlightened about shrinking so that other people won't feel insecure around you."[1]

What's the secret to becoming more confident? Don't try to *act* more confident; *become* more confident. Stop comparing yourself with others.

When you see someone in a group who appears more confident than you, it's easy to feel inferior. When you feel inferior, it's easy to act like you're secure when you're not. You believe you've convinced the other person of your confidence because you've played that role so many times. But they sense that something's not right. They might not recognize it on a conscious level, but they usually detect the presence of a counterfeit.

Here are seven signs that you're truly confident:

1. *You'll stand up for what you believe*—not because you need to be right but because you're not afraid to be wrong.
2. *You're a power listener.* You're much more interested in what others have to say rather than forcing your own opinion.
3. *You're intentional about encouraging others.* You observe people closely and give them the right word at the right time. People get better when they've been with you.
4. *You're open to asking for help.* Insecure people don't want to appear incompetent, but confident people are honest about their shortcomings.
5. *You don't wait for others to make things happen for you;* you simply, quietly take steps to make it happen, with no fanfare.
6. *You don't gossip.* Insecure people put others down so they're higher in comparison. You see others as fellow travelers.
7. *You keep going.* Hardships aren't barriers; they're opportunities to find new pathways.

## Next Steps

You might ask, "Is it really possible to walk away from 'fake confidence' and develop the real thing?" Absolutely. No matter what our patterns have been in the past, we can pick a new direction for the future. If faking it has been a lifelong pattern (especially if trauma-based), it might take professional help—but it's always possible. There is always hope.

How can we change our attitude? By changing the way we think. Our attitude is fluid, not fixed. We can choose it, and we can change it. James Allen wrote, "Every action and feeling is preceded by a thought."[2] The thought comes first; the feeling follows. If we want to change our feelings, we start by changing our thoughts.

Have you ever tried to stop a feeling? If you're mad, sad, or glad, it's tough to simply say, "Well, I'll just stop feeling that way." The energy of the emotion is still there, and we can't simply wish it away. Don't try to change your feelings; change the way you think, and your feelings will follow. King Solomon said, "As a man thinks, so is he."[3] We become what we think about.

Want to become a different person—someone others are attracted to because of your attitude? Pay attention to your thoughts. When you're feeling negative, stop and ask yourself these two questions:

1. What are the facts in this situation?
2. Can I do anything to change the situation?

If you can do something to change the situation, then take action. If you can't change the situation, focus on changing your mindset.

- You're embarrassed at a mistake you made in public and believe everyone is being critical. Remind yourself that you look at your own actions more closely than anyone else, and those actions are probably just a blip on other people's radar.
- Your kids are several hours late, and you're assuming they've been in an accident. Challenge those thoughts by

listing other possibilities that could be much less serious—especially those based on past experience.

- You feel out of control, and it's unnerving. Recognize what you do have control of and focus on that. For the things you can't control, practice accepting the reality and adapting to it.

Developing genuine internal confidence doesn't happen overnight. It requires practice, learning, and sometimes the help of others. If you develop genuine confidence, you'll never have to worry about becoming arrogant. You'll build a healthy foundation that will allow you to confidently impact all your relationships. When you're truly confident on the inside, people will sense it on the outside.

It's a combination of *internal security* and *deep caring for others.*

That's where the journey starts—and it grows one step at a time.

# 12

# Building Block #4— Crafting Integrity

## *Live an Honest Life*

If you have integrity, nothing else matters. If you don't have integrity, nothing else matters.

Unknown

What's the one phrase you never hear in a movie theater anymore? "Wow—how did they do that?"

Years ago, special effects blew our socks off. We'd see a car drive itself, a skyscraper explode, or a jetliner crash, and think, *That didn't really happen, but they sure made it look real!*

Not anymore. With computer-generated imagery, we don't ask how they did it. We know how they did it. We're impressed with the technology, but we're not amazed anymore.

I was presenting a seminar at a major motion picture studio a few years ago. During lunch, I sat with a young man and asked him what he did.

"I work on the web," he offered.

I said, "So you're an internet guy?"

"Nope," he said. "I work on the web. We're filming the latest Spider-Man movie, and I'm in charge of the web that launches from his hand—making it look realistic and natural when it flies out in front of him."

"How do you do that?" I asked.

"Well, we go up on the roof of the tallest building on the studio lot and throw a big ball of yarn off the roof over and over. We digitally film it, so we've recorded the natural impact of the wind, gravity, stuff like that. Then we use the computer to turn the yarn into a spider web, and it looks realistic." Fascinating.

The same thing is true of photographs. We used to see prints of famous people in compromising situations, and it was proof that something had actually happened. Now, our first thought is, *So, is that real, or did someone do digital editing to make it look real?*

When used properly, photo editing software can create something that looks so real we can't tell it's been altered. Used correctly, it can clean up distractions that take away from the focal point in a photo. Used manipulatively, it looks real, but someone deliberately set out to deceive.

As people pleasers, we're experts at personal editing. We've learned what people want to see, so we "edit" ourselves to meet their expectations. We change our words and our behavior to project an image we want others to believe. We think we're impressing them. But nobody is amazed at our lives. Nobody walks away after conversing with us and says, "Wow—how do they do that?"

They've all grown accustomed to people living retouched and edited lives. They rarely see real people in real relationships living lives of integrity. When they do, they assume it's fake. It's the standard they've learned to expect.

## The Slow, Steady Growth of a Dishonest Life

We don't set out early in life to be dishonest. We don't say, "I want to live a fake life so nobody knows who I really am." We want a happy, satisfying life and will do whatever it takes to make that happen. We want people to know us and love us, just the way we are.

The problem is that, as kids, we see tiny opportunities to tweak the truth to get the results we want. It seems simple and innocent at the time, especially if we don't get caught. We're not very good at it at first, as we get caught with cookie crumbs on our shirt while saying, "It wasn't me." But instead of learning not to take cookies, we learn to brush off the crumbs. It's easier and has less consequences than telling the truth.

If we're looking to the opinions of others for our self-worth, it's easy to keep up the pattern of little lies until it becomes a tapestry of dishonesty. It happens so gradually that we don't recognize how much it has become part of our lives. We justify it to ourselves because of the results.

A few years ago, I was part of a small group. One evening, we were given what seemed like a simple challenge: "Can you go a whole day without lying?"

*Piece of cake*, I thought. *Once I've made it through the day, I can give a good report to the group, and they'll think well of me.*

The next morning, I had a phone call with a client who was concerned about an issue. I wanted my company to deal with that issue, so I reported it. "I've had *several* clients who've been concerned about this issue," I said.

It wasn't several clients. It was *one*. But if I said "several," the chances of my company responding would be higher. Technically, I didn't lie. I *exaggerated*. But still, I purposefully tweaked the truth, and I knew it. I misrepresented reality in order to manipulate the outcome.

That was eye-opening. But it got worse. I caught myself ready to exaggerate *six more times* that day. Exaggerating had become my default setting, and I didn't even know it. Telling the exact truth took intentional effort.

Sound familiar?

- Have you ever told someone you appreciated their input but really didn't?
- Have you ever told someone you couldn't meet with them because you already had something planned, but you didn't and really just didn't feel like meeting with them?
- Have you forgotten your spouse's birthday but told them you were planning to surprise them with dinner? (But you just made that up.)
- Have you told someone most of the truth but omitted a key point or two that might make you look bad?
- Have you ever lied to yourself? ("I'm not addicted—I can stop anytime.")

In an earlier chapter, I described how my stories in seminars got better over time, and I had to reel them back in to keep my integrity. What my focus on that problem did, gradually, was to make me more sensitive to it happening. It took my habit of exaggerating out of the background and put it in the foreground.

I'm still amazed at how often I'm prone to spin the truth a bit to make myself appear better to others. When I don't do something I said I would do, I want to make an excuse to cover my laziness or procrastination. The difference is that now I recognize it happening almost every time, because I made that initial commitment to integrity. I don't always make the right choice, but at least it's on my radar instead of hidden from my conscious mind.

Nathaniel Hawthorne wrote in *The Scarlet Letter*, "No man, for any considerable period, can wear one face to himself and another to the multitude, without finally getting bewildered as to which may be the true."[1]

Integrity is an accurate mirror we can use to see ourselves honestly and clearly. In the movie *Something's Gotta Give*, Diane Keaton's character storms out of a restaurant after finding her man (played by Jack Nicholson) having dinner with another woman. He chases after her to explain, and a heated argument follows. At one point he says, "I have never lied to you. I have always told you some version of the truth."

Keaton responds, "The truth doesn't have versions, okay?"[2]

Integrity is the foundation of every healthy relationship. If it's missing, it doesn't matter how many books we read or what advice we follow or what seminars we attend. It doesn't matter if we buy flowers or chocolate or say all the right things. If our integrity suffers, the relationship will *never* thrive long-term. It will decay like termite-infested lumber—looking great on the outside but becoming more and more decayed on the inside.

The most important thing a recovering people pleaser can do is to commit to a life of integrity. It sounds impossible when the opposite has been a lifelong pattern, and it doesn't happen by just thinking, *OK, I'll simply be honest from now on.* It happens by becoming aware of tiny choices we make in which we're tempted to compromise and then making the right decision.

## Tiny Choices That Change Everything

Several years ago, I did some consulting for a utility company. We were talking about how tiny choices lead to huge results. It didn't take long for this group to get the concept, because they had just gone through a real-life example.

One of their software engineers worked so far behind the scenes that nobody ever thought to check up on what he was doing. One of the programs he developed took payments and applied them to accounts. He knew that when the billing was done, the exact charges often ended with a fraction of a penny, so if the calculations said the customer owed $38.45½, the computer would round up their bill to 46 cents. The company got that extra fraction of a cent on the bills of hundreds of thousands of customers each month. This engineer tweaked the program so that instead of the company getting those fractions, they would be diverted into a hidden account for himself.

The company got exactly what it should from its customers and the customers never asked for their fraction of a cent back. The program pretty much ran itself, and there were no safeguards to keep it from happening. It was foolproof. Nobody could find out, since he was in charge of the program.

The mistake he made was bragging about it to a trusted friend, who reported him. I don't know how long he carried out his project. But at the time of his arrest, his hidden account was valued in the upper five figures.

I think there's a lot we can learn from that (other than not to steal from our company or customers).

- Tiny choices, repeated often, yield huge results.
- Bad little choices turn into bad big habits.
- Good little choices turn into good big habits.
- Want to accomplish something huge? Take tiny steps and never stop.
- Want to avoid major pain in your life? Tiny choices count, so choose wisely.

We are what we do repeatedly and over time. *Every choice counts. Every day.*

## Everyday Honesty

People pleasers who are trying to build a solid foundation for their life need to recognize when they might be compromising their integrity and not even realizing it. They're trying to break long-time patterns of casual deceit, so it's important to recognize when there's a problem.

When my wife and I were first married, we lived in a tiny house in Redondo Beach, California. We landscaped the little yard and noticed an interesting young plant that just appeared one day. I didn't know what it was, but it was pretty; bright green serrated leaves that looked like someone's fingers spread from their palm. It grew well, and I took care of it like all the other plants in our yard. Soon it was one of the nicest-looking shrubs in our landscape.

Sometime later, we had friends over for dinner. They were people from our church—good friends we would often hang out with. One of them was a cop.

We had worked hard on our house and were proud of our landscaping. So we took them on a tour. We showed them the flowers and shrubs. We told stories of tearing up the lawn, adding sprinklers, and perfecting the thick, lush lawn they were standing on. Then we took them around to the side yard to continue the tour.

"So, whatcha got here?" our policeman friend said as he approached our accidental plant.

"I don't know—but it's really pretty, isn't it?"

"Yep. Real pretty. Did you plant it?" he said.

"No, it just sprouted one day. It looked cool, so I've been taking care of it."

"You know," he said, "maybe it would be better if you didn't take such good care of it."

"Why not?"

"It's *pot.*"

He did a little research and found out our neighbor had been busted a few months earlier. His yard was full of the plant, which was illegal at the time. Authorities had cleared his yard, but some seeds were still in the ground.

We thought we were great gardeners. Everything we planted grew well; even the things that grew accidently grew well. The marijuana just appeared. We hadn't questioned it but just assumed it was OK.

A lot of things seem to "just appear" in our lives, including thoughts, habits, or attitudes we didn't plant. The people around us might have nurtured a subtle arrogance, pride, or a flair for "innocent" sarcasm in their own lives, and these snuck into our lives too when we weren't looking. It's easy to assume they're harmless, so we let them stay—and water and nurture them. But over time, they take root and grow into full-grown plants.

They might look pretty, but they're dangerous—and are damaging our lives. We need to quit watering them. We need to dig them out.

The only way we can grow is by focusing on the things that help us thrive while intentionally eliminating the things that hold us back.

## Living an Amazing Life

What would happen if our lives actually were amazing? What if we didn't need to pretend to have integrity because we really had it? People would be blown away.

Will Rogers once said, "Live your life in such a way that you would not be ashamed to sell your parrot to the town gossip."[3]

Integrity means that the person you are on the outside matches the person you are on the inside. It means you don't live an edited life.

For a recovering people pleaser, this would be *amazing*!

# 13

# Building Block #5— Strengthening Communication

## Master the Tools of Connection

The ability to speak several languages is an asset, but the ability to keep your mouth shut in any language is priceless.

Anonymous

Do you ever feel ignored during one-on-one conversations? You're talking, but others aren't listening. They ask you a question, and you begin to answer. They're looking into your eyes, but you sense they're a million miles away. Maybe it's their lack of facial response. Maybe it's the quick glance away, distracted by something else. Maybe it's when their next statement has nothing to do with what you just said.

It happens when your teenagers first learn how to roll their eyes. It happens when you're in a meeting and give your input, and nobody acknowledges your contribution. You feel like you're talking into thin air. Sometimes it's an occasional isolated conversation. Other times, it's a pattern.

When it happens repeatedly, you think, *What's wrong with me?* You know you can't force people to pay attention to you. You want to have good communication skills, but there's only so much you can do if others don't cooperate.

For a people pleaser, it can feel like there's no solution, and it'll never change. But once you understand the reasons and factors contributing to these communication frustrations, you can take some simple steps to regain your voice with others. You'll be able to gain their engagement without having to change your personality or become a hard-core extrovert.

The key is to focus on the things you can control in order to build healthy communication patterns. Let's look at them in the context of three key issues that make up those patterns.

## Three Options

When we feel like people don't listen to us, it's natural to take it personally. If we had something valuable to say, they'd listen, right? Since they're not listening, *we* must be the problem.

Actually, there are three options:

1. It could be their problem.
2. It could be our problem.
3. It could be a communication problem.

And most of the time, it's probably a combination of these factors. Here are some things to consider in each case.

### When it's their problem

Other people might not listen to us, and it might not have anything to do with us.

- They could be tired.
- They could be distracted.
- They could be going through a challenging personal journey.
- They could be a person who's not very expressive with their feelings.
- They could simply not be interested in what you're talking about.

It's dangerous to make assumptions about what others are thinking. We interpret their actions and responses based on *our* perspective—but it's important to consider *their* perspective.

If it's a pattern with them, they could be a "toxic" person. No matter what we say, they're in their own world. They're narcissistic—which means that if it's not about them, they have trouble being interested. If they listen, it's not to hear your point of view; it's their chance to plan what they're going to say next, and they need to prove that they're right (and you're wrong).

Any time our self-worth is based on someone else's behavior, we're in trouble. We can influence others, but trying to change them is usually an exercise in futility.

### When it's your problem

You're at a social event, and someone tells you that you have broccoli stuck in your teeth. It's embarrassing, but at least you know. Once you know, you can do something about it—and you're grateful they cared enough to point it out.

Communication is like that too. We can have "blind spots" about how we communicate that everyone knows but nobody tells us about. If we don't know, we can't fix it.

People pleasers who are introverts often feel they can't change anything because it's "just who they are." While it's true they can't change their basic temperament, they can make changes in their communication skills to capitalize on that quiet personality.

Extroverts can be people pleasers too. They are more outgoing and comfortable in their communication but end up offending others because of their insensitive remarks. They also might feel like it's just who they are, but they can become more aware and sensitive in conversations with others.

The good news is that we can make changes in ourselves. But in order to change, we have to know what the problem is.

### When it's a communication problem

When people don't listen to you, it doesn't mean you have no worth. It might mean you don't realize you're using some ineffective techniques.

1. *You don't look for connection.* You're holding up your end of the conversation, but you're not looking for common ground. You make it about you, not about them.

2. *You overexplain.* Even if they're interested, their attention will wane if you're giving point-by-point details. Conversations work best with an "executive summary," not the entire book.

3. *You interrupt.* When they're talking, you think of something that happened to you that relates, so you tell your story. If they haven't finished their own story, you've put the attention on you instead of them. It comes across as rude and implies that you think your stuff is more valuable than what they were saying.

4. *You go down rabbit trails.* What you're saying starts out OK, but you take one point in a different direction, then another—until you're completely off track and they can't follow you.

5. *You don't have a learning attitude.* If you think you're right all the time, it sends the message that you think

they're always wrong. Healthy conversation is a dialogue, not a monologue.

6. *You're usually negative.* When people realize you'll give a worst-case scenario to anything they say, it sucks the energy out of any conversation.

7. *You're sarcastic.* Humor is a powerful tool, but sarcasm is a high form of humor—and a tough one to use well. It usually comes across as passive-aggressive and drives others away from meaningful connections.

8. *You're too loud/soft/fast.* People have different capacities for absorbing information. If they have to work too hard to catch it, they'll eventually stop listening.

These common problems don't reflect on your personal worth; they're just little pieces of broccoli that can get in the way. Recognizing them is the first step toward fixing them.

## How to Get People to Listen to You

It's critical to refocus and see the communication patterns as the problem, not a statement of your own lack of worth. With a few simple techniques, you can immediately see and feel greater connections when you're with others.

Try these simple steps:

- *Keep your side of the conversation simple.* Make one point, explain it briefly, and then ask for their thoughts.
- *Do a time check.* When you call someone or drop into their cubicle, always start with, "Is this a good time?" If it's not, reschedule. Give them a timeframe and ask when they might be available. "What would be a good time for you? I'll just need ten minutes." Then end promptly at the agreed-upon time. They'll be more

inclined to meet in the future when you keep your commitments.

- *Make it about them.* Your stories and ideas have great value, but make sure every conversation brings value to the other person as well. When you show interest in them, they'll be much more inclined to show attention to you.
- *Listen to others without judgment.* Typically, we listen better to people we agree with. When you disagree with someone on something, explore their position without trying to change them. If you listen for understanding instead of planning your response, it builds respect.
- *Don't say "and" so much.* Share one idea at a time, and only one topic per sentence. People get overwhelmed when there's too much to process and respond to.
- *Ask questions instead of giving advice.* It allows the other person to explore their feelings, and they'll learn to trust you. When they're ready for your advice, they'll ask. If they haven't asked, it's premature.
- *Stay focused.* Anything that distracts you from giving your complete attention becomes a barrier to connecting. One example is to put your cell phone completely out of sight. If it's sitting on a table next to you, it's almost impossible to ignore when it vibrates and a text appears on the screen. Sure, you might just glance at it. But the other person notices you're not giving them 100 percent.
- *Be intentional.* When you're silent, it might feel like you're listening—but the other person doesn't know it. You might also be thinking so you can respond. If so, let them know so they don't feel ignored. Asking relevant, clarifying questions based on what they're talking about shows you're being intentional about understanding them. They sense that if you weren't listening, you wouldn't have been able to come up with those questions. A genuine,

intentional interest involves real give-and-take, not just trading talking and silence.

- *Be patient.* Never look at the time during a conversation. An innocent glance implies, *OK, I'm here, but I'm partially focused on what's coming next.* If you truly are on a tight schedule, tell them exactly what your timeframe is before the conversation starts. Then, while they're watching, set the alarm on your phone to go off when it's time. Turn on the ringer and pocket the phone. They'll know it's coming, and you have no reason to check the time until the alarm sounds.

- *Be curious.* Practice approaching conversations with an open mind. The more expectations you have, the harder it will be to listen. It's fine to have an agenda for the conversation, but focus on hearing their response. Listen for the emotions behind their words.

- *Be positive.* When someone shares their opinion, be careful not to minimize their position. Unless they ask, don't critique what they've said. If they want your thoughts, it's OK—but emphasize that you're just sharing your perspective. You don't have to agree with them on everything; you just want to understand what they're thinking.

## How to Read Someone's Mind

There's one communication barrier that's generally more pronounced with people pleasers than other people: assuming you know what someone else is thinking and making decisions as though it were true.

One day early in our marriage, Diane was unusually quiet. She wasn't smiling, and her eyes just weren't quite "right." The day before, we'd been talking about our finances and weren't agreeing.

We never resolved it, so I assumed her quietness the next day was because she was frustrated and angry with me.

Since I decided she was angry, I started thinking about what we had discussed. I narrowed it down to one key issue that was a sticking point for us and decided that's what she was mad about. I got defensive, feeling it was unfair for her to be upset. I started thinking of all the ways my position was right and hers was wrong.

Then I got quiet too—because I was upset with her. After all, how could she shut me down like that without knowing all my reasons? I withdrew (my default setting), waiting for her to say something. As soon as she did, it would be my target—and I could deliver my well-crafted arguments.

She didn't bring it up. That made it worse, because I assumed she didn't care enough about our relationship to talk.

Finally, I knew I needed to say something. "You're awfully quiet today," I said with carefully veiled sarcasm.

She said, "I don't know what I ate last night, but it really didn't agree with me. I feel horrible."

Not what I was expecting. Then it got even worse.

"You've been quiet yourself, but I know you're just giving me space. Thanks for not pushing. I really appreciate it."

I'd made assumptions about what she was thinking. Because I didn't have the facts, I made them up—and they became my reality. I thought I could read her mind. I was wrong.

Psychologists have a word for this: *misattribution*. It means believing you know things about someone without hearing from them and assuming they should know things about you without telling them.

Mind reading is dangerous in any relationship. It bases communication on assumptions rather than facts.

There's only one foolproof way to find out what another person is thinking.

Ask them.

It takes practice, but healthy communication only happens when all the cards are on the table.

Learn to ask, "Tell me what you're thinking," and then listen without responding. You might hear their thoughts, or they might share feelings. Either one is OK. The goal is to understand, not to convince. Make it safe, and you'll build a foundation for serious growth.

## Getting on Other People's Radar

Would you like people to listen to you? Don't focus on what you may think is wrong with you; focus on how you communicate.

Your effectiveness in pleasing other people comes from your ability to communicate well. Fortunately, communication isn't a skill you either have or you don't; it's something anyone can learn and develop. The more you practice, the greater your connection can be with others.

As a people pleaser, you have more potential to become an effective communicator than most people. You've had plenty of practice focusing on others; it's just been with the wrong motive. You've tried to make others feel good about themselves so they'll like you. Now, you're doing it because *you* feel better about yourself, which gives you the resources to genuinely reach out to others—for their benefit.

You'll move from just communicating to genuinely connecting!

# 14

# Building Block #6—
# Fostering Curiosity

*Maintain a Thirst for Wonder*

A conclusion is the place where you got tired of thinking.

Unknown

Have your most important relationships become stale?

- Your marriage used to feel exciting, but it's starting to feel routine.
- Your relationship with your sister or brother has always been energizing, but lately it's become too predictable.
- Your small group of friends meets often for coffee, but the conversation feels stagnant instead of supportive.
- You feel like you have little in common anymore with your parents or your teenagers.

- You have trouble reading your boss's or coworkers' reactions, and you're wondering if they're feeling negatively toward you.

Sound familiar? You're not alone. It happens to all of us. Even the best relationships can get musty over time.

When it happens, it's easy to accept the reality that "the honeymoon has to end." We assume that relationships just get stagnant over time, and there's nothing we can do about it. Mundane becomes the norm, punctuated by occasional bursts of energy.

But it's not true, and it's not necessary. The quality of our lives really comes from our relationships. If our relationships are stale, our accomplishments don't mean much.

People pleasers have developed systems to get approval. These are repeatable ways of approaching people in order to get them to respond in a certain way (they think), so they use those systems every time. They usually don't try anything different because they're exhausted. People pleasing can be a lot of work, so why add more?

On one hand, it sounds like people pleasers aren't very creative. They're locked into one way of doing things. On the other hand, they're more creative than most. They're constantly studying the reactions of other people and developing those systems to get what they need. They're creative because they have to be in order to survive.

The downside is that their life becomes boring. Things always happen the same way, so there's nothing new or exciting. Over time, pleasers can drop into anxiety or depression, feeling resentful that they're working hard to please others while nobody is trying to please them. Their systems aren't effective, and their emotions begin a slow, downward spiral.

It doesn't have to be that way. One of the foundational tools people pleasers can use to take their lives back is to reach beyond the ordinary. They need to become *curious* about how to be creative in building relationships.

## You Are a New Person Today

When you woke up yesterday, you were one person. But throughout the day, you changed. You became a different person because of:

- Conversations you had that made you think differently.
- Things you ate that impacted your body and mind.
- Experiences you had that steered your thinking.
- Choices you made that affected your outcomes.
- Feelings you experienced that you didn't have the day before.

Every day, you change. Imperceptibly, perhaps—but you are different. It's been happening your whole life.

Right now, you are the accumulation of all your life experiences up to this point. Some have been positive; some have been negative—but all have impacted who you are. Tomorrow you'll be different again. So will your spouse, your boss, your kids, your neighbors, and everybody in your life. The change occurs so slowly you don't notice it happening. It's easy to assume that people are the same as they were a week ago—or a year ago. The longer you're in a relationship, the more you're convinced that you know that person well.

But you don't. They're changing. If you don't see it, then you know them less than you did before. And that's dangerous, because you start taking others for granted.

When a new baby comes into your life, you don't know her at all. She's brand-new. You study her constantly, trying to learn who she is. You're learning what she likes and dislikes, how she reacts to things, and what her temperament is like. You're a student of that baby. Over time you get to know her really, really well.

You're *curious.* You're intentional about learning new things about her. When you stop being curious, you assume she's not changing at all.

I have a few friends from high school I stay connected with on Facebook. They're really great people, and I'm grateful for the chance to stay in touch.

But it's been decades since I've sat down and talked with most of them. If you asked me to describe one of them, I'd describe them the way I remember them. But I know they're totally different today because of how life has changed them over the years. I'm different, and so are they. And so are you.

When your relationship with someone begins to go stale, it's probably because you're not seeing the changes that are taking place. You're seeing them the way they were, not the way they are. What happened? You stopped being curious.

If you believe they're not changing, you settle for boredom. But they *are* changing. Stay curious about them, and two things will begin to happen:

- You'll be energized to learn something new about them.
- You won't need to manipulate their opinions of you because you'll be too busy having a real relationship.

## How We Lose Our Curiosity

Kids are naturally curious. If you've spent any time around four-year-olds, you know how many times they ask, "Why?" Because of that curiosity, they explore. When they discover how to do something, they repeat it over and over again. Nobody forces them; they do it for the sheer enjoyment of discovery.

Most adults have lost that curiosity. We get busy with our lives and our work, and we don't have time to investigate. After all, what we're doing is working; why would we want to consider doing it differently?

So, where did we lose it? I think it often happens when kids try to be curious but it's not a positive experience for them.

From a psychological perspective, there are three main reasons kids quit being curious.

*Fear.* If a child doesn't feel safe in their environment, they don't have a secure comfort zone to return to after they've been exploring. A family crisis makes kids uncertain, so they hang tight to whatever they can just to survive.

*Disapproval.* If parents show disgust when their child comes in with muddy shoes, for example, the kids will quit digging for earthworms and exploring the ground.

*Absence.* When parents have their back, kids feel safe roaming. But when parents are physically or emotionally absent, those kids lose the foundation from which they can explore their world. They also don't have anyone to share their discoveries with, which is what encourages them to stay curious.

What can we do to build and maintain a lifestyle of curiosity? Try some of these suggestions to exercise your "curiosity muscle."

1. *Practice curiosity.* When you're driving home from a familiar location, take a different route. Order something new every time you go to a restaurant. Remind yourself that you're doing it to see what else is out there.

2. *Ask open-ended questions that allow you to think.* Don't ask your spouse, "How was your day?" Instead, say, "Tell me something you learned today that you didn't know yesterday." Instead of asking your teenager, "Who's your best friend?" ask, "What is it about your best friend that makes you want to hang out with them?"

3. *Affirm others when they demonstrate curiosity.* "That's such an interesting perspective. I love it when you observe things nobody else sees."

4. *Take a walk* in a crowded area of your city and listen for sounds that are not manmade—like birds chirping, water running, or the wind blowing through trees. Explore the value of listening and simply observing the environment.

5. *Ask journalists' questions about everything:* who, what, where, when, how, and why.

6. *Don't stay bored.* If you're bored, acknowledge it but use it as a trigger to explore something. Help others develop that same pattern.

7. *Show others that it's OK to fail.* Failure means you've learned one more thing that doesn't work, so you're that much closer to success. Fail, then keep moving forward. That's a skill you'll use the rest of your life.

8. *Demonstrate the value of asking good questions.* Make it safe for others to risk answering—and safe if they're wrong as well.

9. *Limit media input.* Television can be educational—but it's simply receiving content, not whetting your appetite to explore and question your world.

10. *When others share discoveries with you, don't add your knowledge to it.* Let it be their moment. Ask probing questions about what they've shared, so they'll want to explore more—and share more.

## Get Curious

Albert Einstein said, "I have no special talents. I am only *passionately curious.*"[1]

What if you took a relationship that was important to you and approached it with renewed curiosity? What if you approached each conversation as an opportunity to really discover what's new in that person's thinking, and how it happened?

No matter how long you've known someone, never assume you fully know them. Every day you're together is an opportunity to explore the mystery of each other's changing inner world. Consider that relationship that's so important to you. Instead of thinking, *I know them inside and out*, try thinking, *They're different today, just a little. I want to find out what that difference looks like.*

When they tell you about something that happened to them recently, ask questions to dive a little deeper.

"So, what did you think when that happened?"

"Then what?"

"How does that change your perspective on that person/ event?"

"How does that change the way you feel? What does that look like?"

"What are you going to do?"

The exact questions don't matter, as long as they're an expression of your genuine curiosity. Their answers allow you to see them through a different lens—*their* lens instead of *yours*.

The best way to love someone is to be curious about them. Taking the time to see the world through their eyes is an incredible expression of compassion. You won't have to try to get them to like you; they'll be responding to your care, not your crafted image.

If your relationships become stale, your life feels stale. It's common to accept that as the way relationships work over time. Don't settle for that. You have a powerful tool to pump life back into those routine relationships: *curiosity.*

## Don't Overlook the Wonder

Anyone who has taken a subway has encountered street musicians. Sometimes they're great. Sometimes they're not. But they're always interesting.

I've seen them on the sidewalks in San Francisco. One young man, probably ten years old, wore an ill-fitting suit and tie while he squawked a few notes on his trumpet. The coin-filled case in front of him held a sign of explanation: "Help me get trumpet lessons."

No matter the quality of the musician, one thing remains the same: almost no one stops to listen. People avoid eye contact, talk on their phones, and rush to their next appointment. Some appear irritated because the music is too loud or annoying (meaning the sound interfered with the music coming through their earbuds). Others are so used to it that they couldn't even tell you someone was there.

Occasionally, someone will slow enough to drop a few coins in their case. There might be one or two who pause for a few seconds and listen—but they soon rush on with their responsibilities.

But what if the musician was really good? Would we be curious enough to stop? Would we allow a little beauty into our day, or would it be crowded out by busyness?

The *Washington Post* decided to find out. In 2007, they put Joshua Bell by the entrance to a subway station in Washington, DC. Simply stated, he's one of the best violinists in the world. A virtuoso. He usually earns about $1,000 per minute when he plays.

And he was playing a 1713 Stradivarius violin worth $3.5 million.

Joshua wore a long-sleeved T-shirt and baseball cap and stood next to a trash can. For forty-five minutes, he played six intricate classical pieces.

In total, 1,097 people passed by. It took six minutes for anyone to acknowledge his presence, until a middle-aged man slowed slightly, looked for a moment—then resumed his pace. A line of people waiting to buy lottery tickets a few feet away produced no glances.

In forty-five minutes, only seven people stopped and listened for even a few seconds.

For Joshua's efforts, he collected $32 in change.

There was one person who tried to stop and listen, craning his neck and twisting to get a better view. His name was Evan, and he did everything he could to get to Joshua and hear the concert. He instinctively knew he was in the presence of greatness. But he couldn't. His mom kept dragging him by the hand, because they were late.

Evan was three years old.[2]

We're busy. We're doing important things, talking to important people, and attending important meetings. We have important places to be and important deadlines to meet. Are we missing greatness that's right in front of us?

It might not be a virtuoso playing a priceless instrument. It might be a child's voice. Or a spouse's heart. A bird's song or a simple flower. It might mean being curious enough to slow down and listen to our own thoughts. Or just to listen, period.

Poet W. H. Davies wrote,

> What is this life if, full of care,
> We have no time to stand and stare?[3]

There's greatness all around us. Let's slow down a bit today and become curious enough to find it.

If we're too busy with our important stuff, we'll miss the wonder.

# 15

# Building Block #7—
# Sharpening Focus

## Pay Attention without Distraction

A person who chases two rabbits catches neither.

Confucius

Suppose I wanted to make my friend Will ineffective. Which of these would be the best way to do that?

1. Get him involved in a serious vice like gambling or drugs.
2. Give him twenty different opportunities, all of which are interesting to him and promise to make him successful.

The first sounds obvious because it could ruin his life and his relationships. But the second is really the most dangerous because it's all good stuff.

In today's culture, most people know we should avoid big vices. But when there are so many opportunities to make a difference, we can't decide which one to focus on. We don't want to say no to any of them, so we dabble in them all. The result? We become ineffective by spreading our energy over a lot of good things.

People pleasers tend to be the most overwhelmed people. Since they're constantly scrambling to get the approval of others, they're hypervigilant about anything they could do to make that happen. That means they've trained themselves to react instantly to every opportunity. Their to-do list never ends.

Most people would say, "Well, you can't do all that stuff. Just take most of them off your list and only do the important things." But a people pleaser sees *all* of them as important. Their lifelong pattern is to determine what to do based on what other people want, not what's important to them. They do a lot of little things, but nothing that helps them become healthy and grow the seeds of genuine relationships.

Developing the ability to focus is critical for becoming a healthy people pleaser who truly makes a difference in the world.

## Does This Apply to Me?

In my day job, I've taught people how to make choices that will give them control of their time and energy. I've specialized in time and life management, teaching seminars about personal effectiveness. I'm supposed to be the expert. I've helped thousands of people, and they've found freedom from the tyranny of the urgent.

But I'm not immune—and neither are you. If we're not vigilant, we become the plumber with leaky pipes at home, the mechanic whose car doesn't run, or the doctor with poor personal health habits.

We have to keep paying attention. Otherwise, the second law of thermodynamics takes over, which says that a moving car will slow down over time if we don't keep our foot on the gas. If we don't take control of our schedule, our schedule will take control of us.

For a people pleaser, distractions can sabotage any efforts to make a difference in the world. Focus sets us up for success.

When I started teaching time management back in the '80s, the whole focus was on "how to get it all done." We carried paper planners and made daily to-do lists, prioritizing each item and working on the important things first.

That need to organize our lives is still true today, but the lists have become overwhelming. It's not about getting it all done anymore, because we simply can't do everything that's in front of us. It's about choosing which things to do. That's tough because all of the options seem good and essential.

It's even worse for people pleasers who want to make an impact in the world. They believe that the more good things they do, the more impact they'll have. So they're driven to do it all. But in the process, they end up being ineffective. They've lost their focus and diluted their impact. It's like trying to stop a burglar by throwing a handful of rice at them.

The sharper the focus, the greater the impact.

If someone throws a ball at us, we instinctively try to catch it. But if they throw two balls at us, our focus is split, and we only give 50 percent of our attention to each one. We end up missing both of them.

## Less Is More

When you wake up in the morning, is your mind already operating at full throttle? You haven't even gotten out of bed, but your mental to-do list jolts you awake like a swarm of hornets. Anxiety grabs you by the throat and says, "C'mon, let's get moving . . . there's stuff to do, and you're already behind."

It might have started hours earlier, robbing you of rest. (Ever notice how much worse everything seems in the middle of the night?) It sets the tone for the entire day. Instead of feeling energized about the day, you just want to grab a spoon and a carton of ice cream for breakfast.

This is not a great way to start the day. You might not experience this often, or maybe it's a daily occurrence. But we've all been there—and it doesn't feel good.

The solution might seem counterintuitive, but the key for making an impact as a people pleaser is to do less, not more. When we're feeling overwhelmed, most of us try to work harder and be more disciplined. But if we haven't triaged our priorities, we'll never dig out from the bottomless, never-ending pile of tasks.

Author Gary Keller shares his personal experience in his book *The One Thing*. He chronicles the massive growth in the results his team achieved by simply cutting down the number of goals they were focusing on. They started with about a dozen—then reduced that by half. Then they narrowed their goals down to three. Each time they narrowed their focus, they saw greater results.

Finally, they picked a single goal. It was the one that, if they achieved it, would make everything else pale in comparison. Their results multiplied exponentially. Keller said, "Extraordinary results are directly determined by how narrow you can make your focus."[1]

It goes back to the 80/20 rule, which says that 80 percent of your results (impact) come from 20 percent of your activities. Or, as Keller said, "A majority of what you want will come from the minority of what you do."[2]

## Dealing with Distraction

You go to the grocery store just to pick up milk. You walk out of the store with chips that were on sale, cupcakes you saw on the clearance rack, and your favorite cheese.

When you get home, you realize you forgot the milk.

Or you need a specific piece of information from an email you read yesterday. You sit down at your computer to find it, and twenty minutes later you've responded to three urgent messages, clicked a link to a Facebook post, scrolled around there and watched a funny video, then took a quick peek at Instagram to see what's new. When you start to get up, you realize you never got the information you needed, and you have to start all over.

When hundreds of things vie for our attention, it's hard to stay focused on what is most important at that moment. Advertisers craft messages and create packaging to capture our attention, whether we're at home or in a shopping mall. It's like a sinister plot to keep us scattered by surrounding us with shiny, noisy distractions.

It works, and it impacts everyone, not just people pleasers. People are more distracted than ever by things that are more enticing than ever. We don't need better time management, because time can't be controlled. We need *distraction management*.

It's easy to assume that high-performing people are just better thinkers than low-performing people. Their brains must work differently, so the rest of us are doomed to lesser things. But it's not true.

Research has shown that our brains are surprisingly similar. Most people have roughly the same amount of storage available—and it's massive. We can hang on to an amazing amount of information. But we *all* have a very small workspace. That workspace is where we focus our attention. If there are too many things in our workspace, we lose our ability to pay attention.

Think of it as the desk in your office. It's designed to be for *work*, not *storage*. It's where you get things done. When that desk has piles everywhere, it's hard to concentrate. There are too many things to catch our eye when our current task gets hard.

You might say, "Yeah, I have a messy desk—but I know exactly where everything is." That's great. But that's treating your desk as a storage place instead of a workspace. The problem with a messy desk isn't the clutter; it's the potential for distraction.

Our mental workspace is the same way. It's a small desk used to get something done, not to store a bunch of other stuff.

## You're No Einstein

When people think of "smart," they often think of Albert Einstein. He pondered the universe and came up with things like the theory of relativity. I asked some friends what the theory of relativity was, and nobody could really explain it. They knew they'd studied it in school but couldn't remember it beyond having to know answers for the test.

We assume Einstein was smart because we don't understand him. We say, "He thought at a whole different level, and it's beyond me. So he was way smarter than me." Or maybe it was his hair. People who think deeply might not have time left over for grooming.

The problem is that we see what he (and others like him) accomplished and think, *I could never do that. I don't have much to contribute.* That's why people often say, "I'm no Einstein."

It's true. You're not Einstein. Never have been, never will be. You can't make the contribution he made. You're *you.* You can make a contribution nobody in the universe can make. If you don't make it, you're robbing the world of that contribution.

So, what's the difference between you and Einstein?

For one thing, *Einstein didn't have email.* Seriously. The reason he came up with such great ideas was probably because he didn't have as many distractions.

Bring him forward a few decades to the present day. Imagine Einstein sitting at his desk, pondering the universe. But he gets stuck on an idea and isn't sure where to go with it. So he checks his email. Or Facebook. Or he tweets his friends and reads their posts. He tries pondering again, but his thoughts about the universe still don't go anywhere. So he grabs his smartphone and plays a couple hands of solitaire. Just for a few minutes, of course.

Little distractions keep us from being focused. But more than that, they take our momentum. It takes a while to ramp up again after each one.

I don't think Einstein was that different from us. We have the potential to make a universe-sized contribution that nobody else could make, including Einstein—as long as we don't get distracted.

What's something significant you've been working on, something that could really make a difference if you figured it out and finished it? Something that's hard enough (but important enough) that it takes energy and focus? When you put time into it, how often do you get distracted? And what are you distracted by?

What would happen if you could control the distractions? *It could change everything.*

Einstein was probably just a focused version of us. In fact, he once said, "It's not that I'm so smart; it's just that I stay with problems longer."[3]

Ready to make a difference?

Put the smartphone down slowly, back away, and nobody will get hurt . . .

(By the way, Einstein had a simple way of describing the theory of relativity: "When you are courting a nice girl, an hour seems like a second. When you sit on a red-hot cinder, a second seems like an hour. That's relativity."[4])

# 16

# Building Block #8— Practicing Self-Care

## Invest in Yourself

Almost everything will work again if you unplug it for a few minutes, including you.

Anne Lamott[1]

I have a group of friends who get together to play a board game called Settlers of Catan. They make whole evening events of it, bringing snacks and spending hours on strategy.

A lot of my people pleasing friends might think they're wasting time, because they're not doing anything productive. "I'd never be able to do that," they say. "I can't take time for myself because my to-do list is so long. I wouldn't be able to enjoy it, and I'd feel guilty the whole time we were playing."

My friends don't see it that way. It has value to them. I told them I thought it was a cult. Actually, I'm just jealous because

I'm not smart enough to keep up with them. (I find Chutes and Ladders challenging.)

So, who's right? Are they wasting time, or not? Am I wasting time when I watch a hockey game on TV? When I go out for coffee or lunch with friends? When I take a long walk just to think instead of exercising hard?

Matt is a teacher and has a short lunch hour. When we get together for lunch, it takes more time to drive there than we get to spend together. Is that a waste of time?

Some people want to be superproductive all the time. If they're not getting results, they feel like they're wasting time. For them, every moment has to have some type of productive outcome. As Tim Hansel wrote in his book by the same title, "When I relax, I feel guilty."[2]

So, what determines if time is wasted or not? If it provides value for me or someone else.

Downtime isn't wasted when it

helps me recover from a hectic schedule;

restores my energy, my focus, and my capacity;

provides true enjoyment rather than just mindless activity;

allows me to create; or

gives me more in return than the time I spend on it.

*Creativity can't be rushed.* Imagine telling Michelangelo to hurry up and paint the Sistine Chapel faster.

*Relationships can't be rushed.* Taking time is the only way relationships can be built. Time with people isn't time spent—it's time invested.

When we waste something, we throw it away. It has no value to us or anyone else. When we invest in something, the return is multiplied. If we weigh time on the scale of productivity, downtime will always be a waste. If we weigh time on the scale of relationships and renewal, downtime will always be a wise investment.

*Downtime prepares us for uptime.* It's great to be productive and make great accomplishments. But for a people pleaser, the tendency is to do that so others will think favorably of us. We're constantly overwhelmed because there's no "neutral" setting in our lives—only "drive."

This building block is the most overlooked for a people pleaser, because it focuses on ourselves. When we're operating from a paradigm that finds our value in the opinions of others, it feels more important to invest in them than ourselves. When that's our focus, self-care just seems wrong.

In reality, taking care of ourselves is the most important thing we can do if we're going to please others effectively. It's like the flight instructions to put on our own oxygen mask before helping others. If we put others first, we'll soon lose the ability to help them at all.

Investing in ourselves is a skill that can be learned, and its benefits are almost immediate. The tough part is changing our mindset to believe it's worth the effort.

## Three Steps to Investing in Yourself

Changing a lifelong paradigm is new territory for people pleasers, so we need a simple, repeatable, step-by-step process. It's something we make choices about, then continue the process as we start seeing results. Think through each of the following steps and how you can begin to apply them to your own experience.

### 1. Build on the past.

"If your house caught on fire, what would you take with you on the way out the door?"

We've all heard that question, and we all have similar answers:

- Family members and pets
- Photo albums (pictures of family members)

158

- Special mementos (things made by family members that have special meaning)

I don't know anyone who says, "I'd grab the couch," or "I paid a lot for that ceiling fan—it's coming with me." If we can replace it, we leave it behind. What we paid for it doesn't matter. The value doesn't come from the cost; it comes from the relationship it represents. We rescue the things that are irreplaceable—the things that connect us to others.

My wife has crafted photo albums that cover our entire marriage. They include hundreds of pictures of the things we've done together, of our kids and grandkids, of our friends. They show special events and significant moments that have brought us to today. With the comments she's added, they represent a journal of our lives.

Whenever someone wants to know about some event from the past—when something happened, who was involved, what we were doing—she grabs the appropriate album. Within seconds, we have the answer we're looking for.

But it doesn't stop there. We then find ourselves browsing through a few other pages as old memories capture our attention. "Hey, look at that! Remember when you had those sideburns? And that curly perm is crazy! I don't remember your hair being that color . . ."

We're reminded of memories we had forgotten—and that's a good thing. It's not healthy to live in the past, yearning for the "good old days," but the richness of life comes when our past provides meaning for our present. That's why we study history; remembering where we've *been* gives context for where we *are*.

On our deathbed, we won't be focusing on the colors we picked for our living room. We'll think about the conversations we had in it. We won't think about how our yard was landscaped; we'll think about the people we played games with out there. The vacation scenery won't matter as much as who came with us on the trip. We'll remember the people we made those memories with.

Why is this important for a people pleaser? Because we tend to ignore the past as being all about getting what we wanted from others. We focus on the present for the same reason. With a healthy approach to people pleasing, we can focus on the present to build genuine memories that will have value in the future. We'll look back on today and find joy.

### 2. Check your inputs.

The late speaker and author Charlie "Tremendous" Jones said, "Five years from now, you will pretty much be the same as you are today except for two things: the books you read and the people you get close to."[3]

I'm not sure how instrumental that quote was in developing my perspective about life. But hearing quotes like that shaped my love of reading and conversation.

I think it goes like this:

- We become what we think about.
- What we think about comes from our inputs.
- Our inputs come through our senses—especially what we hear and what we watch.
- We can choose what we hear and watch.

If I understand this correctly, then the ingredients that form my thoughts are:

- The conversations I have.
- The things I read.
- The things I watch.

The logical conclusion? If I want to be better than I am, I need to be choosy about those ingredients.

There are a lot of things trying to get my attention. Advertisers yell at me from billboards when I'm driving. They interrupt story lines of my favorite shows with commercials. They talk to me through little screens at the gas pump, trying to convince me that I need their credit card or to come inside and grab a snack. Hundreds of thousands of new books are published every year. My inbox is filled with requests from people who want something from me. Flyers are tossed onto my doorstep, stuck under my windshield, or handed to me in a crowd as people try to find creative ways to get me to *look*.

These are not all bad. In fact, there are great things to read, watch, and observe. But there are too many to choose from. I can't take them all in. If I'm not intentional about those inputs, I'll end up selecting the shiniest ones. Those ingredients will begin to shape my thinking—which will shape my life.

You can't prepare a healthy snack if the only ingredients you have in your cupboards are sugar, butter, and chocolate. It might be tasty, but not healthy. You need different ingredients to get different results.

So, how do you sort through the inputs to make sure you get the best ones?

1. Determine who you want to be.
2. Determine what ingredients will get you there.
3. Intentionally select the best ingredients.

High-quality ingredients produce high-quality results. Good-quality ingredients produce good-quality results. Low-quality ingredients produce low-quality results. It doesn't happen any other way. If you want a high-quality life, you need to be choosier about your choices.

### 3. Live in the moment.

I tend to live for tomorrow, though it's not my intent. I know we're supposed to take one day at a time. But I have a long to-do list. (You too?) So when I tackle something on that list, my focus isn't usually on the task itself. I'm not thinking about what I'm doing, savoring the moment, and experiencing each event. I'm fulfilling the expectations of others so I don't disappoint them. I'm trying to finish so I can move on to the next thing, getting me closer to the end.

I get check marks. But I miss the moments.

Most people live for check marks. We spend most of the year charging forward, trying to catch up and stay ahead, then we look forward to taking a vacation to recover. But on that vacation, we use our unpressured time to catch up on our emails.

We miss the richness of life by living ahead of ourselves, and we're always looking over our shoulder to see how other people are responding.

It's like a parent who videotapes every moment of their kids' parties and special events. But when viewing them later, they see their kids—never themselves with their kids. By preserving the memories for the future, they miss being part of those memories.

Here's the unsettling truth: When you die, there will still be more to do. Make sure you do the important stuff.

If we have a long list of people we're trying to please each day, we're focused on getting through our list—and nobody feels special. We're driven by our list instead of our relationships.

My son-in-law, Brian, is all about living in the moment. He's in sales, and he could sell a fur coat to a wooly mammoth. But that's not because he has advanced sales training or special techniques. It's because the person he's with gets his full attention. The relationship is genuine, and people buy from him because he's fully present when he's with them.

That's rare. We're not used to people engaging with us without being distracted. It's refreshing when they do.

Look at your to-do list: Are you living for today or for tomorrow? What if you took each item and tried to experience it fully and undistractedly?

Here are five ways to be fully present.

1. Don't look at electronics while in any conversation, whether one-on-one or in a meeting. Set your phone down where you can't see it until you're done.
2. Set appointments for your technology. Decide how many times you'll check your email each day and put those appointments on your calendar. Be fully engaged in technology when it's technology time, and fully engaged in people when it's people time. Don't let them get mixed together.
3. Be aware of your environment. Whether inside or outside, notice the details of your surroundings. Take time to listen to the sounds around you. Observe the little details you would normally miss; feel the temperature and the breeze. Listen for sounds that aren't manmade.
4. Turn off the radio in your car. Take time to think instead of having constant input. If it feels uncomfortable, it's probably a sign that there's a problem.
5. Don't let a totally organized environment be your top priority. Nobody cares if you die with an empty inbox. They care when you've made a difference in their life.

## Take Care of You

If our value comes from what other people think, we'll need to please other people. If our value comes from inside ourselves, we'll need to please ourselves. For a people pleaser, that sounds selfish and self-defeating. That's why this building block is more than a change of how we operate.

It's a change in how we think.

Pleasing others in meaningful ways will happen in direct proportion to how much you invest in yourself.

# 17

# Building Block #9—
# Developing Gratefulness

*Search for the Positive*

Piglet noticed that even though he had a very small heart, it
could hold a rather large amount of gratitude.

A. A. Milne[1]

When Diane and I first got married, we didn't have a lot of money.
We rented a tiny house in Redondo Beach, California. Tiny, meaning 450 square feet. That was it. It's what we could afford.

It was a fixer-upper, and we saved rent by agreeing to do some
repairs and restoration ourselves. We worked together to put in a
lawn, paint the house, and install flower beds and plants. It was
a lot of work, but we didn't care. We were in L-O-V-E, and we
did it together.

The house was only a few blocks from the beach, so we'd often
walk down there in the evenings. It didn't cost anything, and we
could just hold hands and talk. We couldn't afford to go to the
movies or out to dinner often—but that was OK.

We were just grateful to be together.

For our wedding, someone gave us several large, heavy boxes for a gift. When we opened them, they were filled with dozens of cans of food—but someone had taken all the labels off. "What a clever gift," we said. We laughed because it was so random.

We tucked those cans away in the top shelf of our kitchen cupboard, wondering what we would ever do with them. At least up there they were out of the way.

But in that first year or so of marriage, there were more than a few times when we ran out of money and the refrigerator was empty. So we would select three cans, shaking them to guess what was inside. We would set them on the table with a can opener and say grace over them—thanking God for our meal.

Then we'd open them. It wasn't unusual to have a meal of canned peaches, beans, and olives.

I don't think we would ever go to a restaurant and order that combination. But we remember those meals—not because of the randomness of the food but because of the gratefulness we felt for provision. It was there when we needed it, and we never took it for granted.

At the time of this writing, we've been married forty-three years. There have been ups and downs in every area of life—but we've worked hard to stay grateful. All the cans in our cupboards have labels today. When we plan a meal, we know exactly what's coming. There's something comforting about that.

*But it's not nearly as exciting.*

At the beginning of a relationship, most people have more time than stuff. Later in a relationship, most people have more stuff than time.

Stuff isn't bad. But it's easy to take it for granted when we have a lot of it.

Time is good, because it's where we live. But it's easy to let time get crowded out by stuff. Maybe it's time to think back to the beginning.

- What was your relationship like when you had more time than stuff?
- How is it different now?
- What choices could you make to find more time in your relationship?
- How can you become as grateful for the present as you were for the past?

A typical people pleaser has a mindset of scarcity. Since they shape their sense of value by the opinions and approval of others, they feel good whenever someone affirms them. But it's never enough. Ten people could affirm them and one person ignore them—and their focus is on that one person. They can never be grateful because their goal is to have *perfection* in how many people approve of them.

Healthy people pleasers have a mindset of abundance. Their sense of value is personal and internal, whether or not other people express approval. They're thankful for the people who affirm them, but they don't need it from everyone.

*They're grateful.*

It's a mindset that sets them up to impact others, allowing them to give rather than just take. And it applies to every area of their life.

## Cultivating Gratefulness

Changing the way we think might seem impossible, but it's usually a matter of simple choices that move us in a new direction. Like a seedling that's planted, it doesn't grow full-sized overnight. We make a choice to water it daily and fertilize regularly. If we skip a few days, the plant shrivels. If we keep up the daily pattern of watering, it thrives and develops exponentially over time.

Cultivating a mindset of gratefulness doesn't mean we ignore the painful things that happen. We've been hurt by others, and that hurt is real. Gratefulness recognizes that reality but actively focuses on the things that are positive as well.

There's an old country song about having your heart stomped on and mashed flat. Got anybody in your life who did that? It's usually somebody you trusted. You've had a long relationship with them and consider them to be a friend. You've enjoyed their company and shared life together. They might even be a family member.

But they turned on you. They talked about you behind your back. Or they confronted you about an issue they've had with you for some time but never told you about. You weren't expecting it, and it caught you completely off-guard. They said or did something that broke your trust.

*They stomped on your heart.*

The American Thanksgiving holiday is usually a day when routine is broken up with family, friends, feasting, and football. You might be conscious about being thankful because you're "supposed to," so that's where your focus is. You intentionally think about the things you're grateful for and maybe even share them around the dinner table. You're distracted from your hurt feelings.

The next day, you're back to the routine, and you're feeling your sore heart again. Should you still be thankful the day after Thanksgiving? And a week or month later?

*Yes.*

Thanksgiving Day is a chance to practice something we should do every day of the year. But it's not because it's an obligation so we'll "think positive" and "have a good attitude." It's because gratefulness is the only way to keep from becoming a victim of the people and circumstances in our lives.

We all know people who've been hurt over the years and have allowed that hurt to poison their lives. They're bitter. They would say, "What do I have to be thankful for, anyway? Look what they've done to me. They've ruined my life."

Gratefulness is the antidote to that poison. Here's how it works:

- *It gives us perspective.* When the hurt is huge, it's easy to ignore the reality of the positive things in life. Choosing to be grateful helps us to see both elements realistically.
- *It doesn't minimize the pain.* The hurt is real, and we can't ignore it. It doesn't help for someone to say, "You just need to get over it." I had a lot of pain after surgery recently and told my doctor about it. "Of course it hurts," he said. "Somebody cut you with a knife. It's going to hurt while it's healing. But it won't hurt as much over time, even though the scar is there." Gratefulness helps with healing.
- *It keeps us from being a victim.* Someone once said, "No one can mess up your life unless you give them permission." If we focus indefinitely on the injury, we give away the control of our emotions to that person. Developing an "attitude of gratitude" helps us stay in control in the long run.
- *It keeps our emotional energy where it belongs.* There are people in our lives who need our time, attention, and emotional investment. They deserve it. Bitterness drains that energy away, so there's less available for those people. Thankfulness keeps our reserves high.

There are no easy answers to tough relationship problems. People mess up our lives, and it hurts. There might never be a resolution, and the relationship may never be healed. The pain they caused might need the attention of a trained professional to sort through.

But at this point in the process, the easiest way to begin to heal is to choose to be thankful for everything we possibly can. It's not a cure-all solution, just a way to be realistic about the life we're living.

## Imperfect Gratefulness

When I arrive at a hotel in the morning to teach a seminar, the meeting room is usually set up and ready to go. Tables are in place and covered, the audio-visual system is set, chairs are arranged, and coffee is brewing in the corner. A crew has come early in the morning to make it all happen.

Then they disappear. Those people are trained to be invisible—to work in the background. That's unfortunate, because they can make or break an event. The amazing work they do means I don't have to worry about that stuff. If my seminar goes well, their fingerprints are all over it.

Once in a while I run into one of them and make it a point to express my gratefulness. We often speak different languages, but that's OK. We just make a human connection, and they know I appreciate them.

A few weeks ago, it went the other way. When I arrived at the hotel where I was training their staff, in Arizona, the room was set up perfectly. But someone had written a message on a flip chart at the front of the room. It simply said, *Well Come Guess.*

At first, I thought someone had forgotten to tear off that sheet from a previous session. But after a few minutes, I realized it was a message to me from one of those invisible workers. They wanted to express their appreciation for my using their meeting room and felt the need to say hi.

That hotel provided some of the best customer service I've ever encountered. The worker didn't care that their message might not be in the best English. They wanted to express their gratefulness and leave a greeting anyway.

After a bit I finally realized what the message was intended to say: *Welcome, Guest!*

When I pointed it out to the manager of that team, she smiled and nodded. "That's typical," she said. "They're so excited to serve people that sometimes they just can't help themselves.

169

They're grateful you've given them the chance to serve, and it just leaks out."

What a great reminder. My tendency is to make sure I do things perfectly and express myself with exactly the right words. If I can't do that, I just skip it. I figure it's a little thing, and it doesn't matter that much.

It does. To them. But if I keep gratefulness inside, it never helps anybody. I need to learn to put spoken gratefulness over perfection.

*The most imperfect connection is better than the unspoken one every time.*

### Choosing Gratefulness

People pleasers often have an unrealistic view of life. They see someone who seems secure with themselves and others and say, "I wish I could be like that." It looks like the other person is living a perfect life, so it's easy to get dissatisfied with their own life.

Comparison is always a losing game because it makes us ungrateful.

Occasionally, my wife and I will walk through the model homes of a new housing development. It gives us the chance to do something we don't do in normal life—walk in the front door of somebody else's house without knocking and wander around from room to room. (I'm guessing that if we tried that in our neighborhood, we might get to explore the back seat of a police cruiser.)

I've noticed that while we're walking through these homes, everybody whispers. It's like we're trying not to disturb the occupants, even though we know there aren't any.

The houses are clean. Music is playing softly. There's no clutter. The garage is empty and immaculate (that's how I know no one lives there). Storage space is everywhere. There are no scratches on cupboard doors, no dust on top of the television, no smudges on the windows. There are no dirty dishes in the sink. There's no mortgage. The homes are beautiful.

*And they're sterile.*

There's no clutter of real life. There are no echoes of kids playing, no footprints of love on the carpet.

These houses aren't lived in. They're for show. We think, *Wow, if we had this house, our lives would be as peaceful as it feels here.* But eventually those houses sell, and people move in. The garages fill up, sticky fingerprints show up on appliances, and crayons color the walls.

That's what houses are for. They're not for display; they're containers for real life and real relationships. If they're for real life, they have to be used. It's like the old children's book about the velveteen rabbit—he was a stuffed animal that had to be loved by a child until his fur was worn off before he could become real.

Model homes are nice places to visit. But our own homes are where life and love happen. It's easy to take them for granted. Maybe today would be a good day to be grateful for our imperfect homes—and the people who make them imperfect.

Gratefulness disappears when comparison shows up. We see what we don't have in terms of relationships, affirmation from others, and "stuff," and we get discouraged. Gratefulness is a choice we make, and it has to be intentional. When we practice that choice repeatedly, gratefulness grows and becomes the filter we use to look at life.

Try it tomorrow morning. Don't get out of bed until you've thought of three things you're grateful for. Write them down. The next day, pick three different things. Do this for a week. If you do, you'll find this practice impacting your attitude about everything else in your day.

Make every day Thanksgiving Day. Maybe you'll get your heart back.

# 18

# Building Block #10—
# Keeping Perspective

*Accept Reality*

When we are in awe of something bigger than we are, it makes it easier to focus on others.

Paul Piff[1]

The newspaper said it would either be the greatest meteor shower ever—or it wouldn't happen at all.

I've always been a fan of outer space, so anything that happens up there gets my attention. When Saturn is in the evening sky, I pull out my telescope to study its rings. The five moons of Jupiter always capture my interest. I've studied enough full moons that I could probably find my way around up there without having to ask for directions. I never get tired of watching the International Space Station glide across the sky, even though I've seen it hundreds of times.

Meteor showers are special. They don't happen very often, so I've set my alarm for sometime after midnight and stood in my yard many times. It's often cold, and my neck hurts from staring straight up.

It has never worked. All I get is a stiff neck and insomnia. It's probably because I live in Southern California, so there's too much light. It's tough to see many stars, much less a meteor shower.

But when a friend texted me about this one, I allowed myself to hope. There were two things that would be different about this one.

1. Based on a mathematical formula, it had the potential to be the greatest meteor shower ever (or a complete dud).
2. It would occur while I was staying at a cabin in the mountains above six thousand feet, and there were no streetlights.

So, at 12:30 a.m. I bundled up and went outside. It was cold and crisp, and the loudness of the wind blowing through the forest was uncanny. Looking straight up, I could see the black silhouettes of the treetops dancing against the star-crusted sky.

I stood there for about ten minutes. There were no meteors. I thought, *OK, just one. If I can just see one meteor up here, I'll be happy.*

That one never came. Finally, I heard myself say aloud, "Well, that's a disappointment."

Immediately, I realized the irony of my statement. I didn't see any meteors, so I was disappointed. But that whole time *I had been so focused on the missing meteors that I had overlooked the majesty above me.*

Usually, the sky I see at home is black with occasional stars perforating the blackness. But here it seemed to be the opposite. There were so many stars that the black night sky seemed to recede into the background. I hadn't seen that many stars since I was a kid, looking out the car window as my parents drove through the Arizona desert in the middle of the night.

So there I was, focused on the most amazing scene and saying, "Well, that's a disappointment."

I do that more often than I realize. I go through life looking for a unique, exciting event but miss the everyday miracles while I'm doing it.

There's majesty all around us—in nature, in our relationships, in our opportunities, in our faith, in our jobs, in our conversations, in our passion.

Meteors are great, but they're unpredictable. Let's enjoy them when they come but not count on them. It's too easy to miss the majesty.

The *Macmillan Dictionary* defines *perspective* as "a sensible way of judging how good, bad, important, etc. something is in comparison with other things."[2] It means when we look at things, we assume that what we see from our vantage point is accurate. But when we move to a different position, we see it from a different angle. It doesn't change the original perspective but adds to it.

My dad used to say, "Well, in my humble but absolutely correct opinion . . ." I knew he was joking, because he was a good listener and rarely saw his own view of things as the final word. But I also know how common that perspective is with many people. After all, if we're looking at something, it seems obvious that our perspective is correct because it's right in front of us.

People pleasers are often threatened when someone has a different perspective than they do. They've found a view of things that works for them and don't want to consider other viewpoints. Being in control versus being open to other perspectives is part of their security. I heard a speaker once say, "If I think I'm right, do I really want your opinion?"

World-class people pleasers have learned how to take a few intentional steps back in order to see things in relation to everything else. They know what they perceive but want to see how it fits. That's why perspective is an important building block for someone who wants to impact others from a place of healthy self-worth. They base their perspective on reality, so they're constantly challenging their viewpoint to see how they can make it multidimensional. They might not see meteors, but they change their perspective so they don't miss the sky.

People who have perspective are looking for truth, and they're not threatened by others who think differently. They're willing to listen to others—not to change their minds, but to look through their eyes in order to clarify their own perspective.

## The Value of Weeds

This building block of perspective can be understood just by looking around us. The simplest examples in everyday life demonstrate how to make that mental shift. A good example can be found whenever we try to landscape a house or plant a garden.

There's something about gardening that's good for the soul. It's one of those things where we participate in the process but can't force the results. We plant the seeds, provide the water and nutrients, trim, prune, and protect. We supply the right conditions and the plant grows all by itself.

As the saying goes, "Gardening is cheaper than therapy, and you get tomatoes." If we're good at our part, we have a "green thumb" (because everything turns green). If we're not very good, we have a "brown thumb" (because everything turns brown).

I'm a little of both. Over the years, I've had some success with a few plants. A lot of others, not so much. But there's one thing I'm really good at growing: *weeds*.

By that standard, I must have a green thumb because my weeds grow so well. Evidently, I'm providing just the right amount of water and nutrients and putting in just the right amount of effort, because those weeds grow fast and multiply like crazy. They're full, they're lush, they're healthy.

Some time ago, my daughter sent me this definition of a weed (I'm a little uncertain what prompted her to look it up).

Weed: A plant that is not valued where it is growing, and is usually of vigorous growth.[3]

That got me thinking. A weed is a plant just like any other plant. It grows "vigorously," which is just what we want plants to do. It's just in the wrong place.

If we've worked hard to have a perfectly manicured lawn, we wouldn't want flowers growing in the middle of the yard. Flowers are beautiful, and they might grow vigorously. But we want them in a flower bed. In the lawn, those flowers would be considered weeds. They'd be in the wrong place. If lush grass was growing in our flower beds, it would be considered a weed too. It's in the wrong place.

We plant our yards with things that surround us with beauty and symmetry. We select our plants carefully, choosing the ones that are appealing to us and ignoring the ones we dislike.

Weeds are plants that aren't appealing to us, and they show up where we don't want them to. And they grow vigorously.

*It's the context that determines whether they're flowers or weeds.*

When we drive through the hills near our house in the spring, they're vibrantly green. We're speechless at the beauty. But when we stop and hike through those hills, we realize why: they're covered with weeds. The same weeds we work so hard to get out of our gardens and lawns.

But those weeds are exactly where they need to be, serving a critical purpose: they're preventing erosion, keeping the topsoil from washing away.

Without perspective, I'm upset with the weeds. With perspective, I appreciate them when they're busy holding the hills up. If they show up in my garden, they're toast.

## How to Become an Optimist

Perspective is powerful for a healthy people pleaser because it focuses on reality, not just a single viewpoint. We don't have to assume we're right but have the ability to serve others by exploring their perspectives as well. It means we listen, which is the fastest way to build trust with another person.

World-class people pleasers have learned to change their perspective. They don't automatically believe everything that goes through their head but actively look for the positive side. It's a choice they make, and it's intentional. They don't overlook the negative, but they don't assume that's all there is.

We can choose what we think about. I learned this several years ago while vacuuming our house. To me, the best part of vacuuming is making lines. No matter what direction they go, vacuum lines shout that the carpet is clean. (I've often thought that if I just dragged a stick across the carpet in a pattern, people would think it was freshly vacuumed.)

Over the years I've tried different patterns to make the lines symmetrical or creative or expressive. I almost feel like it's half science, half art. I want people to walk in and see the lines so they know I've cleaned for them.

But it doesn't last long. After a day or so, the lines are gone, replaced with footprints. Usually, when I see the footprints, I think, *Oh, now I have to vacuum again.* It feels like something that needs to be fixed. If the carpet has no lines, it feels like the whole house is out of order.

On one Sunday morning, it was different. As I walked out of the bedroom and looked into the living room, there were no lines. Instead I saw footprints—hundreds of them. It was the exact opposite of the perfection I strive for. Normally, it would have been frustrating.

But this time it made me smile.

They were little footprints, not big ones. They were from the day before when our granddaughters, Averie and Elena (ages six and three at the time), had spent hours with me in that room. Foam blocks had become castles as Averie told nonstop stories of dragons and princesses and kings and moats. Wooden train cars kept Elena occupied as she scooted animals and trees and signs across the tracks. We'd talked and laughed and played until dinner. Mostly, we'd just loved.

The room had been filled with shrieks of delight, with wrestling and pillow fights and "tickle bugs." It was a room of giggles and joys and memories being born.

It's what that room was for.

The next morning, there were no carpet lines. But instead of my usual frustration, I felt a deep satisfaction with what had happed in that room. The footprints were a joyful reminder of what the carpet was made for.

I still enjoy making lines when I vacuum. But when little people are coming, my vacuuming isn't to get rid of the footprints.

*It's to prepare for them.*

# PART 4

# HOW TO CHANGE

Do you ever feel like you're just going through the motions of life each day?

You'd like things to get better, and you have great intentions of making it happen. You get motivated for a while, but then you slip back into old patterns. Changing is like trying to dry yourself with a towel while standing in the rain.

The more this process happens, the more discouraging it becomes. Each failure feels worse than the last one, and you feel like there's no hope of change. Maybe you also feel like you'll always be this way, and it's easier to just accept your position in life than to deal with constant failure. It's a lot less work with a lot less guilt.

Guess what? You're not alone. We've all been there. We want something better, but it seems out of reach.

It's called "being human."

The internet is bursting at the seams with motivational slogans, memes, and challenges. Instagram has entire profiles that focus on inspirational quotes that express what we want to be but haven't yet become. They all provide some version of, "I want that to be me." They're expressions of our dreams and aspirations.

I've never seen a mug that says, "I'm just OK." I did see one once that said, "Dream small—it's your only hope for success, really."

We all laugh because it's true for most of us at one time or another. But it doesn't have to be true for you going forward. This final section focuses on three areas:

- How to change
- Where faith fits
- A strategy for world-class people pleasing

It's a simple message we all need to internalize: *you are enough*. Let's learn how to make that a reality for your entire future.

# 19

# The Secret to Changing Everything

It's never too late to be who you might have been.

George Eliot[1]

What do you feel when you hear the word *change?*

If you're in a situation you don't like, change is a welcome relief. If you're in a situation you enjoy, change can be discouraging—or even terrifying.

Either way, change takes us out of our comfort zones—and we like our comfort zones. We don't want to admit it, because the internet is full of motivational quotes telling us how bad comfort zones are and how great change is. But if we're honest, most of us are comfortable in our comfort zones. That's how they got their name.

It's like sleep. We might love the excitement and energy of each day, but we're compelled to return to the comfort of our pillow every night. It restores us for something different tomorrow.

The key is to recognize that change is going to happen. Maybe not every day, but it's coming. Someone said that at any point in time, we're either in the middle of change, coming out of change, or about to go into change. At the same time, we might feel the need to change—but realize it won't happen unless we make it happen.

External change just happens. Internal change is a choice.

For a people pleaser, that option of choosing can be sweetly terrifying. You've lived your whole life for the approval of others. It's familiar and comfortable, but you know it's sucking your life away. You want to change, but it would move you into new, unfamiliar territory. You're also afraid that the old shackles of people pleasing are impossible to break, and you'll slip back into those old patterns and fail.

External change is inevitable, and we need to live in that reality. Internal change is where we craft our future, and it's something to pursue. Together, these changes can alter our lives.

## The Truth about Comfort Zones

I travel a lot, but I'm not a great traveler. I like the *idea* of travel, but the whole process is stressful. I tend to worry about all the little details of the trip before they ever happen.

- I wonder if my luggage is overweight.
- I worry about making connections if my flight is delayed.
- I stress over whether my carry-on bag will fit in the overhead compartment, and what will happen if they have to check it—and then it gets lost.
- I hope the hotel has my reservation.

My wife and I went to Europe for the first time a few years ago. I worried about getting a cab driver who didn't speak English (which happened) and not being able to direct him to our hotel (he found it anyway). I worried about finding bathrooms in unfamiliar places, eating unfamiliar food, and experiencing unfamiliar experiences. I was way out of my comfort zone.

That trip turned out to be awesome. Nothing I dreaded (except the cab driver thing) came to pass. Now we're talking about going back to Europe. My first thought is to repeat the exact trip since it's familiar. It would be in my comfort zone.

Some people aren't travelers and don't see life as a journey. They've gotten addicted to comfort, which anesthetizes them to the richness found in exploring life. Over time, their perspective on life dims. They shrink inward instead of expanding outward, and they lose their sense of purpose. But whether we're an adventure-taker or an adventure-watcher, most of us have one thing in common: we like our comfort zones.

Is that a bad thing? We've heard for years, "You need to leave your comfort zone." We've been told that real life takes place when we stretch beyond where we are currently and move in new, meaningful directions. It's the refrain of a productivity-driven society. Here's the argument:

1. We were meant for greatness.
2. We're not great now.
3. We need to move away from our comfort zone to become great.
4. We should never be satisfied with the way things are but should strive for something better.
5. If we stay where we are, we're living a mediocre life.

There are a lot of variations on that theme, but the basic idea is the same: *we need to change.*

The first step to change happens when we get a vision of what life can be if we stretch. Our life would be richer, our contribution greater, and our relationships more fulfilling. But many people assume that leaving their comfort zone will take them to a scary, uncomfortable world where they don't speak the language or know their way around. They're OK for a short vacation, but they're relieved when they get home to familiar surroundings.

That feeling is real, and it's OK. We need to *come home* on a regular basis. It's where we regroup, recover, and find our balance. But we also need to *leave home* on a regular basis, moving in new directions and adding value to our lives (and the lives of others).

If we believe that our comfort zone is bad, we'll lose the richness of living in the present. We'll feel guilty whenever we're not stretching, and we'll always be stressed about future performance.

What if we could find a balance: being satisfied with the present (fully engaged in each moment) while taking steps to make a difference in the future? We would experience a quantum leap in our quality of life, with less effort than we expected. We would make a contribution. We would matter.

We don't need to make giant movements. We can go to the edge of our comfort zone, intentionally step slightly outside those borders, then hang out there until it *becomes* comfortable (as part of our expanded comfort zone). Then we repeat the process—stretch, adapt, get comfortable. Then do it again, and again.

It's called growth.

*When we stop growing, we start dying.* Do you find yourself giving up because it's too much work to grow, and you're starting to settle? Stay in your comfort zone but stick your toes out regularly to expand that comfort zone. It's something *anyone* can do—and if you make it a habit, it'll change your life.

Who knows what adventures you'll find?

## The Three Stages of Healthy Change

What does that look like for a people pleaser? Changing from being an unhealthy people pleaser to a healthy one is like being in a boat that's tied to the dock when we really want to sail to Hawaii. A lot of people dream of the destination, but then think of everything that could go wrong on the journey—so they stay put.

Any trip that's worth taking involves three stages:

1. Leaving the dock.
2. Sailing across unknown territory.
3. Arriving at your destination.

In Stage One, we're in familiar territory. It smells like fish, it's noisy, and we have the same routine every day. It's not like Hawaii, but it's safe—because we're tied to the security of the dock. It's tough to leave because we're not sure what the journey will be like. The dock is a "known," while the ocean journey is "unknown."

The task here is to untie the boat, overcome inertia, and start sailing. It doesn't feel as safe, and it's not as comfortable—but it's where the magic begins.

In Stage Two, our senses are heightened. We're much more aware of what's happening around us, because it's new and uncertain and risky. Before long we forget about the dock because we're focused on the challenges of the journey.

Usually, two things happen in this stage.

1. We realize that we have what it takes to meet these challenges. We're facing situations we haven't faced before, and this forces us to draw on our resourcefulness to deal with them.
2. We start getting comfortable with our increased ability, and we come alive just a little bit. We've stretched—and survived.

It's a long journey, and it's new and different. But over time, it becomes the "new normal." Our comfort zone has expanded, and we've grown into it. Discomfort turns into comfort after we've done something for a while.

In Stage Three, we reach our destination. It's time to celebrate and explore. We've left our comfort zone of the ocean and make decisions about this new environment.

*Most people never get to Stage Three because they're afraid of untying the boat from the dock.*

These transitions from stage to stage can feel like a giant leap. But as soon as that leap happens, we quickly adjust to the new routine. It's like getting into a cold swimming pool. When we merely stick our toes in, the water feels like ice. It's warm outside the pool. We try to build up our courage but end up sitting in a lounge chair and sipping something with a little umbrella in it. But if we jump in, two things happen:

1. We feel the shock of reality.
2. We adjust quickly, and within seconds the water feels warm.

Transitions are almost always scary because they're so different from our current situation. But once we enter the water, we realize we have what it takes.

We just have to jump.

## The #1 Resource for Handling Change

People resist change when they focus on what they have to give up instead of what they'll gain. They stay comfortable. They're not sure how to handle the next stage, because they've never been there.

So, do you have what it takes? Absolutely. You are the #1 resource for handling change in your life. You are what it takes for each stage. When you jump into that next stage, you'll find that the resources you need surface when you need them most.

Life is all about change. Sometimes that change is painful. Other times it's amazing. Most of the time it's both.

The key to growth is to keep moving toward change. Whenever you do, the new stage will capture your attention more than the old stage. Eventually, you'll find the future more interesting than the past. That's when you know it's working.

What's the next step? Untie the boat and set sail.

Take the risk to become a healthy people pleaser who can impact the world, one life at a time.

# 20

# The Faith Chapter*

Acting perfect in church is like dressing up for an x-ray.

Unknown

Soon after I had written my first book, another author gave me some simple, practical advice: "Don't read your Amazon reviews."

I didn't see what the harm would be, so I ignored his advice. After all, I was a people pleaser . . . so this was a perfect opportunity to get unsolicited positive opinions from others. I knew the book was good (in my opinion), so I figured all the reviews would be glowing commendations.

Fortunately, most of the reviews were positive. But there were a few people who thought I had missed the mark, and they weren't

*Disclaimer: If you're not a person of faith, feel free to skip this chapter. Everything I've written has been designed to give anyone a path to freedom and power as a people pleaser, no matter what their worldview is. My own worldview comes from a deep faith in God, and it would be dishonest if I didn't add that perspective. In my original people pleasing state, I would have omitted this chapter rather than risk offense. But healthy people pleasing is based on being totally honest, so I'm including it. I think you'll find it thought-provoking, but it's your call. If you decide to pass, I'll meet you in the final chapter!

shy in expressing their opinion publicly. No matter how many good reviews there were, in my mind they were canceled out by the negative ones. Somebody didn't like what I had done and said so in writing. It was pretty devastating.

Now, in my career as a consultant, I've presented thousands of seminars to mostly secular or corporate audiences. I also speak in churches and Christian conferences on a regular basis, but the corporate gig has been my "day job." That's why I wanted to write books anyone could benefit from reading—not just those whom we might call "Jesus followers," people who have discovered a genuine relationship with Jesus Christ that becomes the foundation of their life. My books haven't had a ton of biblical content but just enough that people could recognize my faith-based worldview.

Even though the majority of my reviews have been very positive, that approach has set me up for twice as much criticism, coming from both extremes, about the same book.

> "He barely mentions God or uses Scripture to back anything up."
> "All he did was preach through the whole thing."

Over time, I've realized that it's my job to be honest in my writing and use my own unique approach. If I do that, there will always be a few people who don't like it, no matter what I do. That's OK, because it's not my job to make everyone like me. It's my job to be true to myself and get people to think.

## What Does God Say about People Pleasing?

Most Jesus followers assume that people pleasing is bad. That's why we see so many things online telling us to "quit worrying about what other people think. The only thing that matters is what God thinks about us, and he loves us. Learn to accept that and ignore everybody else and their opinions."

This sounds good, but I think it's lopsided and incomplete. It's based on the selfish version of people pleasing that's only self-focused, when we find our identity in what others think of us. Getting our value from God's view of us instead of our own is exactly what needs to happen. But if we stop there, we might feel better—but we'll ignore others because they've been a source of pain.

We shouldn't stop there. Life is designed to happen in community, not isolation.

Some people say, "I don't need anybody else; God is enough." This also might sound good, but it's unbiblical. God does want a personal relationship with us, but most of the work he does in our lives happens through other people. In Genesis 2:18, God said, "It is not good for the man to be alone." Yes, it's in a specific context, and this verse is often quoted at weddings, but the principle is seen throughout Scripture. We're made for relationship, not isolation. In a sense, we're made for the right kind of people pleasing.

So, what *does* the Bible say? Here are two foundational principles to consider.

1. We need to know how God feels about us, then make that the basis of our self-worth and identity.
   - "We are God's handiwork." (Eph. 2:10)
   - "[Nothing] will be able to separate us from the love of God." (Rom. 8:39)
   - "God demonstrates his own love for us in this: While we were still sinners, Christ died for us." (Rom. 5:8)
   - "The LORD your God . . . will take great delight in you." (Zeph. 3:17)
   - "I have loved you with an everlasting love." (Jer. 31:3)

2. We need to let God love other people through us (healthy people pleasing).

- "Since God so loved us, we also ought to love one another." (1 John 4:11)
- "Carry each other's burdens." (Gal. 6:2)
- "Live in harmony with one another. Do not be proud, but be willing to associate with people of low position. Do not be conceited." (Rom. 12:16)
- "Each of you should use whatever gift you have received to serve others." (1 Pet. 4:10)
- "Do nothing out of selfish ambition or vain conceit. Rather, in humility value others above yourselves, not looking to your own interests but each of you to the interests of others." (Phil. 2:3–4)

God simply adores you, exactly the way you are, whether you feel like you deserve it or not. If God says you have value and you say you don't have value, one of you is mistaken. Guess who that would be?

Once we've developed a healthy foundation of personal worth based on God's perspective, it's expected that we'll become honest, effective people pleasers—doing things with a focus on others that will give them what they need. We won't be using them for our own purposes; we'll be serving them.

## Exhaustion: A Red Flag

Most people pleasers are exhausted from their constant vigilance of what others think and from trying to manipulate their opinions. They might not realize it because it's so familiar—just like we don't think about the air surrounding us. Exhaustion often becomes a subtle "badge of honor," showing that we're really committed to meeting the needs of others instead of focusing on ourselves.

Even if we've learned to find our value in God's opinion of us instead of looking to others, there's a temptation to take serving others to an extreme. We become healthy, and we're ready to serve. But it's easy to get so focused on others that we're worn out. Something about it feels noble and God-pleasing.

That perspective breaks down when we look at the life of Jesus himself. He was busy healing the sick, teaching the multitudes, investing in his followers, and challenging the religious leaders. But on his busiest days, we see him withdrawing from the crowds to restore and renew his soul through rest, isolation, and time with God, his Father.

- "Very early in the morning, while it was still dark, Jesus got up, left the house and went off to a solitary place, where he prayed." (Mark 1:35)
- "Jesus often withdrew to lonely places and prayed." (Luke 5:16)
- "After he had dismissed them, he went up on a mountainside by himself to pray. Later that night, he was there alone." (Matt. 14:23)

Sure, Jesus met the needs of a lot of people, but not everyone. He didn't try to please everyone who wanted his attention, and he left many unhealed. He knew his boundaries and took time for himself instead of making himself available all the time.

We often hear people say we need to "take on his yoke," which means we need to labor in service. We assume it's going to be hard labor and an exhausting process. But Jesus says, "My yoke is easy and my burden is light" (Matt. 11:30). That means that if our yoke is heavy, it's not from God.

In biblical times, a yoke was a wooden device used to connect two oxen so they could work together in a field, multiplying the results of their effort. It was handmade to perfectly fit across the neck and shoulders of the oxen to prevent chafing or cutting. It didn't make their job harder because of its weight; it made their work easier because of its design.

Sometimes accepting an easy yoke is tougher for Christians, because we feel the need to demonstrate to others how faithful we are. We hide our struggles for fear that others won't find God attractive. In reality, our vulnerability is what attracts others, because they can identify with our journey more than perfection.

In 1992, Sheila Walsh was a well-known and respected Christian singer, author, and cohost of a popular Christian television talk show, *The 700 Club*. She became so focused on her image and performance that she forgot to pay attention to her inner world, and it all came crashing down. Here's how she described it:

> One morning I was sitting on national television with my nice suit and inflatable hairdo, and that night I was in the locked ward of a psychiatric hospital. It was the kindest thing God could have done to me.
>
> The very first day in the hospital, the psychiatrist asked me, "Who are you?"
>
> "I'm the co-host of *The 700 Club*."
>
> "That's not what I meant," he said.
>
> "Well, I'm a writer. I'm a singer."
>
> "That's not what I meant. Who are you?"
>
> "I don't have a clue," I said. And he replied, "Now that's right, and that's why you're here."[1]

People pleasing is an image we acquire to feel good about ourselves. But since it's not real, it gradually destroys us from the inside out. Finding our value in reality—in what God says about us—is the first step in a journey to health and wholeness that can impact others.

## Can You Do It without God?

Throughout this book, we've been exploring how to switch from unhealthy people pleasing (making others happy so they'll like us) to healthy people pleasing (finding our value internally so we can reach out to others). This switch makes people pleasing something to strive for by reframing what it looks like. We've also looked at the five fears that get people trapped and how to overcome them, plus ten building blocks to position us to impact others in the best possible way.

Yes, it's possible to overcome your people pleasing ways and find your own personal value by looking in the right mirror. You can learn to be comfortable in your own skin and find the freedom to reach out to others. Anyone can do that, and the steps aren't that difficult. It gives you a life of satisfaction and balance and frees you from your lifelong prison of people pleasing. You can focus on others because you're good with who you are on the inside.

But without first experiencing God's deep love for you and having a personal relationship with him, you'll miss the power that comes with it. The reason we seek approval from others is that we're all created with an insatiable desire to know that we matter. God put that desire in us, and he's the only one who can fill that need.

When you're healthy enough on the inside to reach out to others, you'll live a satisfying life. If God becomes the source of your value, you can change the world.

# 21

# A Long-Term Strategy for Success

Tomorrow (noun): a mystical land where 99 percent of all human productivity, motivation, and achievement are stored.

Unknown

What if you didn't know your limitations? What could your life be like?

Cliff Young was a potato farmer in Australia. That's all he had ever done. He worked the family farm, which was huge—about two thousand acres. They also had about two thousand sheep on the farm. His main job growing up was to herd the sheep. Since they didn't have sheepdogs, he had to do it himself. So he would round up the sheep on foot, running, because it was just the easiest way. Sometimes he ran constantly from dawn until dusk to get the job done. On a number of occasions, he ran for twenty-four hours—all day and night—to prove to himself that he could do it.

He knew he was good at running. It was in his blood. One day, he heard about a race taking place in his area. It was called an ultramarathon, and it covered 544 miles from Sydney to Melbourne. He knew he could go the distance, but he was really slow and had an unusual way of running, almost loping or limping. He had never even seen a professional race—but he decided to try anyway.

The good news? There were only six other participants in the race, seasoned runners who had been racing for years. The bad news? He was sixty-one years old—decades older than the others.

On the day of the race, he showed up wearing his overalls and rubber boots. Everyone made fun of him. But that's what he had always worn to run, and that's how he would run this race. After the starting gun, he was immediately in last place. He managed to keep the other runners in sight for a while, but as the first day progressed, they pulled away and he found himself running alone.

Jump to the finish line. Five days, fifteen hours, and four minutes after he started, he crossed the finish line. He was sure he was in last place. But he was wrong.

He came in first place. And he beat the other runners by two full days.

Later, he found out why. Since he didn't know anything about racing, he didn't know he was supposed to stop and sleep at night. So he kept running with that slow pace and awkward gait—and unknowingly shuffled past his faster, younger competitors *while they were sleeping.*[1]

What would happen if we took our life challenges, watched how other people handled the same challenges, and did the opposite?

Speaker Jim Rohn used to say that we should find someone who had great success—but blew it. Offer them cash and say, "Here's some money. Please teach me everything you did to mess up your life so I can avoid doing it."[2]

I like that. Watching others could be a great resource for moving in some really positive directions.

- Everybody has areas in life they struggle with, and they're not finding success. What if we did the opposite?
- Everybody has dreams, but many have given up because those dreams seem hard. What if we did the opposite?
- Everybody has a challenging relationship that's important to them, but they avoid communication. What if we took the risk and did the opposite?
- Every people pleaser sees themselves as trapped in a pattern, and they want to escape. What if we saw it as a potential positive and did the opposite?

If we do what most people do, we'll get the results most people get.

If we do the opposite of what most people do, we might get the opposite of what most people get.

Is there hope for moving from unhealthy people pleasing to healthy people pleasing? Absolutely, as long as we take the opposite approach from most people and instead follow one like I've outlined in this book.

## Making a Dent in the World

If you suddenly disappeared from the earth, *how many people would notice?* Of the people who would notice, *how many would care?*

The ones who cared would be the people on whom you've had the greatest impact. They're different people because they've known you. The greater the impact, the more they would miss you.

We all have that desire to make our impact grow. We want to make a big difference, beyond just the people we know.

We want to matter.

Some people go through life on a mission to amass great wealth. Their primary focus is making sure they're taking care of their own possessions and security. They can be extremely successful in the process, but it's no guarantee they're impacting anyone.

Other people are focused on others. They can still become extremely wealthy and successful, but it's their secondary motive. To them, success happens when they make a positive impact beyond themselves, such as working for a relief agency or volunteering at a homeless shelter.

*Impact* is when something happens and there's evidence left behind afterward. If a shopping cart rolls into your car in the parking lot, it leaves a dent. Even if someone moved the cart away, you're left with that little dent reminding you your car was impacted.

A single event can make a huge impact on a person.

Some events have a *negative* impact. A car accident, a spouse's betrayal of trust, or a terminal diagnosis changes someone's life instantly and permanently. They're worse off because the unexpected happened, and it was big and it was bad.

Some events have a *positive* impact. Winning the lottery or landing a dream job makes a positive impact, but it wears off over time. That's why most lottery winners end up back in their original lifestyle after just a few years.

Both negative and positive events happen to all of us. They're unplanned, unexpected, and unpredictable. At the same time, you can be intentional about making a difference with others. It doesn't have to be a major event that changes their lives. It's a choice you make—and it's planned, expected, and predictable. You might look at those who are making a massive impact and think, *If I had the time or money or education or connections or skill or situation they have, I could do that.*

The truth is, you *can* make the same kind of impact, but it will look totally different. Your uniqueness is your toolset for impacting others. If you use somebody else's tools, you won't get the same result. Nobody else has your tools or the ability to use those tools in your way. Understanding and capitalizing on your uniqueness is the key to making an impact, which won't happen while you're just trying to get others to like you.

That's the motivation for jumping on the journey toward change: the chance to actually make a difference. It doesn't happen overnight but through a lifetime of little choices. It's tough to just go out and make a big impact, because there are too many variables you can't control.

It's easier to make a small difference right now, right where you are, with whoever you're with. Make a small difference long enough, and it eventually turns into a big impact.

Big impact happens in a slow cooker, not a microwave. And anybody can do it.

*You can do it. And you can start today!*

# The Final Word

If you've spent your life as a people pleaser, living under the constant need to make others happy, this whole process probably sounds refreshing. If it's accurate, it means that freedom is possible.

- You can build a totally new paradigm about yourself, finding your value and worth internally instead of in the opinions of others.
- When that happens, you'll be able to use your people pleasing tendencies to impact everyone you come in contact with.
- You can make a serious dent in the world.
- *You will matter!*

You might still be thinking, *It sounds good—but is it real? What if it doesn't work?*

If you go through the process we've explored, the chance of healing and impact is huge. But if you don't try, you're guaranteeing you'll be trapped in the same place you are now.

Why not try?

Why not now?

*It's your life—make it matter!*

# Acknowledgments

Everybody wants to write a book. No sane person should do so. Ernest Hemingway (and several others) were reported to have said, "There is nothing to writing. All you do is sit down at the typewriter and bleed." It's mostly done in solitude but is dependent on the support of others.

This is my sixth book, and I'm keenly aware now of how vital others are in any writing endeavor. Some of these people unknowingly provided nuggets of ideas. Sometimes they supplied encouragement to continue. Others have simply walked quietly alongside on this solitary journey. Most were all of these.

That list could be pages long. But for this book, a few names rise to the surface: those who have been there and stayed through the end.

Jeff Goins has become my writing mentor and thought leader. The founder of Tribe Writers, he has guided thousands of creatives to achieve their unique purposes and dreams. We connected a couple of years ago when I joined his intimate mastermind group, and he simply allowed me to ride shotgun while he went on his own journey of growth and change. Having that up-close perspective consistently challenged my mindset, and I'm a totally different person because of it. He's unpretentious and cares deeply, and I'm grateful and humbled for his investment in my journey.

There are others in that group with whom I have been traveling, fellow creatives who have become my good friends. We're all on our own unique journeys but have the mutual support of others who "get it." We've all learned the power of community, and we're all better for it.

That means that this book is covered with the fingerprints of Sarah Robinson, Brianna Lamberson, Jessica Whitehead, Lex Latkovski, Ty Ziglar, Lucy Stevens, Dave and Janet Wernli, Annie Beth Donahue, Caroline DePalatis, Eric Gale, Tiffany Babb, Carolina Sizemore, Laura Naughton, Jeff Jackson, Tracy Papa, Tyler Williams, Danie Botha, Seth Guge, Danielle Bernock, Andy Traub, and others. Most of them have no idea how much they have influenced this book by their conversations, stories, encouragement, and simply being there. They're priceless gifts.

Partnering with my editor, Vicki Crumpton, for the sixth time is like having a personal trainer for my words; she takes my raw material and sees the potential—but keeps my voice in the process. Once she puts her virtual red pen on my manuscript, it's the same feeling you get when you wax and detail your car. She knows how to clean it, polish it, get rid of the seagull droppings, and make it shine. Writing has been a joy because of that relationship, and I'm grateful.

Without my wife, Diane, you wouldn't be holding this book. Doing life together with your best friend makes a lot of good things happen inside your head, which puts a lot of good words and ideas in there. I'm able to write because of her, and fully recognize the treasure she is in my life.

Words come together well when there are important people on your journey with you. My family gives meaning, my friends give support, my colleagues give me opportunities, and God gives me himself.

To all of you, I give you my "acknowledgments." You're all a gift, and I value you more than I can express.

Thanks.

# Notes

### Part 1  Building a Vision

1. James Clear, *Atomic Habits* (New York: Avery, 2018), 188.

### Chapter 1  How Did We Get This Way?

1. Philippe Rochat, "Five Levels of Self-Awareness As They Unfold Early in Life," *Consciousness and Cognition* 12 (2003), http://www.psychology.emory.edu/cognition/rochat/Rochat5levels.pdf.

### Chapter 3  How to Spot a Counterfeit

1. Robert Quillen, "Robert Quillen Quotes," *Goodreads*, accessed January 11, 2020, https://www.goodreads.com/author/quotes/5734044.Robert_Quillen.
2. Urban Dictionary, s.v. "people pleaser," accessed June 3, 2020, https://www.urbandictionary.com/define.php?term=people%20pleaser.

### Chapter 4  I Need You to Like Me

1. C. Joybell C., "C. Joybell C. Sayings and Quotes," *Wise Old Sayings*, accessed January 11, 2020, http://www.wiseoldsayings.com/authors/c.-joybell-c.-quotes/.
2. Theodore Roosevelt, "The Strenuous Life," speech at the Hamilton Club, Chicago, April 10, 1899, in *The Works of Theodore Roosevelt*, vol. 13 (New York: C. Scribner's Sons, 1926), 320.
3. Frank Sinatra, "Frank Sinatra Sayings and Quotes," *Wise Old Sayings*, accessed January 11, 2020, http://www.wiseoldsayings.com/authors/frank-sin atra-quotes/.
4. Robert Foster Bennett, "Robert Foster Bennett Quotes," *More Famous Quotes*, accessed January 11, 2020, http://www.morefamousquotes.com/authors/robert-foster-bennett-quotes/.

## Chapter 5  I Need You to Not Be Angry with Me

1. Patrick Lencioni, "Patrick Lencioni on Healthy Conflict," *Success*, February 10, 2015, https://www.success.com/patrick-lencioni-on-healthy-conflict/.

2. D. Donaldson and F. Macpherson, "Müller-Lyer Illusion," July 2017, https://www.illusionsindex.org/ir/mueller-lyer.

3. Jean-Philippe Laurenceau, "Two Distinct Emotional Experiences in Romantic Relationships: Effects of Perceptions Regarding Approach of Intimacy and Avoidance of Conflict," *Personality and Social Psychology Bulletin*, August 1, 2005, https://journals.sagepub.com/doi/10.1177/0146167205274447.

## Chapter 6  I Need You to Notice Me

1. Sonya Sones, *One of Those Hideous Books Where the Mother Dies* (New York: Simon & Schuster, 2013), https://www.simonandschuster.com/books/One-of-Those-Hideous-Books-Where-the-Mother-Dies/Sonya-Sones/9781442493834120.

2. Neel Burton, "Man's Search for Meaning," *Psychology Today*, May 24, 2012, https://www.psychologytoday.com/us/blog/hide-and-seek/201205/mans-search-meaning.

## Chapter 7  I Need You to Affirm Me

1. Kay Wyma, *I'm Happy for You (Sort of . . . Not Really)* (Colorado Springs: Waterbook Press, 2015), 92.

## Chapter 8  I Need You to Need Me

1. Susan J. Noonan, "Volunteer When Depressed? The Life You Save May Be Your Own," *Psychology Today*, June 18, 2016, https://www.psychologytoday.com/us/blog/view-the-mist/201606/volunteer-when-depressed-the-life-you-save-may-be-your-own.

## Chapter 9  Building Block #1—Being Proactive

1. Aaron Ben-Zeev, "Do Only Dead Fish Swim with the Stream?," *Psychology Today*, March 15, 2017, https://www.psychologytoday.com/us/blog/in-the-name-love/201703/do-only-dead-fish-swim-the-stream.

2. James Stuart Bell and Jeanette Gardner Littleton, *Living the Serenity Prayer: True Stories of Acceptance, Courage, and Wisdom* (Avon, MA: Adams Media, 2007), 3.

## Chapter 10  Building Block #2—Staying Connected

1. Maria Konnikova, "The Limits of Friendship," *The New Yorker*, October 7, 2014, https://www.newyorker.com/science/maria-konnikova/social-media-affect-math-dunbar-number-friendships.

## Chapter 11  Building Block #3—Building Confidence

1. "A Return to Love Quotes," *Goodreads*, accessed January 11, 2020, https://www.goodreads.com/work/quotes/1239848-a-return-to-love-reflections-on-the-principles-of-a-course-in-miracles.

2. James Allen, "James Allen Quotations," *Quotetab*, accessed January 11, 2020, https://www.quotetab.com/quote/by-james-allen/every-action-and-feeling-is-preceded-by-a-thought.

3. Proverbs 23:7, paraphrase.

## Chapter 12  Building Block #4—Crafting Integrity

1. Nathaniel Hawthorne, "The Scarlet Letter," *Spark Notes*, accessed January 11, 2020, https://www.sparknotes.com/nofear/lit/the-scarlet-letter/chapter-20/.

2. "*Something's Gotta Give*: Quotes," IMDb, accessed June 3, 2020, https://www.imdb.com/title/tt0337741/quotes/?tab=qt&ref_=tt_trv_qu.

3. Will Rogers, "Will Rogers Quotes," *Goodreads*, accessed July 8, 2020, https://www.goodreads.com/author/quotes/132444.Will_Rogers.

## Chapter 14  Building Block #6—Fostering Curiosity

1. Marcel Schwantes, "This Famous Albert Einstein Quote Nails It," *Inc.*, February 5, 2018, https://www.inc.com/marcel-schwantes/this-1-simple-way-of-thinking-separates-smartest-people-from-everyone-else.html, emphasis added.

2. Gene Weingarten, "Pearls Before Breakfast," *The Washington Post*, April 8, 2007, https://www.washingtonpost.com/lifestyle/magazine/pearls-before-break fast-can-one-of-the-nations-great-musicians-cut-through-the-fog-of-a-dc-rush-hour-lets-find-out/2014/09/23/8a6d46da-4331-11e4-b47c-f5889e061e5f_story.html.

3. As quoted in Weingarten, "Pearls Before Breakfast."

## Chapter 15  Building Block #7—Sharpening Focus

1. Gary Keller, *The One Thing* (Austin: Bard Press, 2012), 10.

2. Keller, *One Thing*, 38.

3. James P. Gray, "It's a Gray Area: Einstein's Brilliant Thoughts Pertinent to Today's Woes," *LA Times*, May 31, 2013.

4. "Albert Einstein Quotes," *Goodreads*, accessed January 11, 2020, https://www.goodreads.com/quotes/9028-when-you-are-courting-a-nice-girl-an-hour-seems.

## Chapter 16  Building Block #8—Practicing Self-Care

1. Erin Clements, "Every Single Thing I Know, as of Today," *Today*, April 9, 2015, https://www.today.com/popculture/author-anne-lamott-shares-life-wisdom-viral-facebook-post-t13881.

2. Tim Hansel, *When I Relax, I Feel Guilty* (Elgin, IL: Chariot Family Publishing, 1979).

3. "Charlie 'Tremendous' Jones," *Tremendous Leadership*, accessed June 3, 2020, https://tremendousleadership.com/pages/Charlie.

## Chapter 17  Building Block #9—Developing Gratefulness

1. "A. A. Milne Quotes," *Goodreads*, accessed January 11, 2020, https://www.good reads.com/quotes/391381-piglet-noticed-that-even-though-he-had-a-very-small.

## Chapter 18 Building Block #10—Keeping Perspective

1. Paul Piff and Dacher Keltner, "Why Do We Experience Awe?," *New York Times*, May 22, 2015, https://www.nytimes.com/2015/05/24/opinion/sunday/why -do-we-experience-awe.html.
2. Macmillan Dictionary, s.v. "perspective," accessed June 3, 2020, https:// www.macmillandictionary.com/dictionary/american/perspective#perspective_9.
3. Merriam-Webster Dictionary, s.v. "weed," accessed June 3, 2020, https:// www.merriam-webster.com/dictionary/weed.

## Chapter 19 The Secret to Changing Everything

1. Rebecca Mead, "Middlemarch and Me," *The New Yorker*, February 6, 2011, https://www.newyorker.com/magazine/2011/02/14/middlemarch-and-me.

## Chapter 20 The Faith Chapter

1. Sheila Walsh, "Who Are You?," *Leadership Journal* (Summer 2002): 52–53.

## Chapter 21 A Long-Term Strategy for Success

1. "The Legend of Cliff Young: The 61-Year-Old Farmer Who Won the World's Toughest Race," *Elite Feet*, accessed June 3, 2020, https://elitefeet.com/the-legend -of-cliff-young.
2. "Jim Rohn—The Formula for Failure and Success," Spotify playlist by John Craig Swartz, track 3, "Learn from Their Mistakes," https://open.spotify.com /playlist/7F197r7OZCC91fNyTMFqiV.

**Dr. Mike Bechtle** (EdD, Arizona State University) is a communications expert, seminar leader, and author of seven books, including *People Can't Drive You Crazy If You Don't Give Them the Keys* and *How to Communicate with Confidence*. His articles have appeared in publications such as *Writer's Digest*, Pastors.com, *Focus on the Family*, and *Entrepreneur*. A frequent speaker, Bechtle lives in California. Learn more at www.mikebechtle.com.

# FOR MORE
## COMMUNICATION TOOLS,
# PRACTICAL INSIGHT,
## AND MOTIVATION, VISIT

### MIKEBECHTLE.COM
  **@MIKEBECHTLE**

# YOU **DON'T** HAVE TO BE CONTROLLED BY
# DIFFICULT PEOPLE!

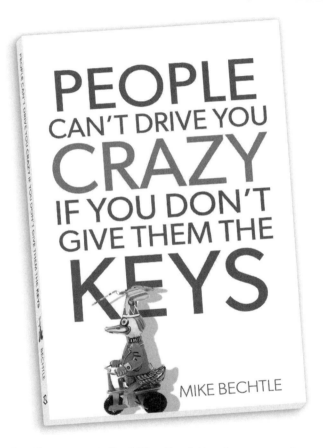

Communication expert Dr. Mike Bechtle shows you how to stop being a victim of other people's craziness. With commonsense wisdom and proactive advice that you can put into practice immediately, Bechtle gives you a proven strategy to handle crazy people—and stay sane while doing it.